What People are saying about Dian Griesel, DGI and her books...

"Dian has delivered yet another straightforward, unfiltered book that is ESSENTIAL! Another masterpiece!"
— *Deborah Solomon, Deborah Solomon LLC*

"If I had to pick one life and business coach, it would be Dian.... No one person can offer her unique skill set for business, the market, media and general well-being."
— *Mark Goldwasser, CEO and President, National Securities*

"Dian Griesel is the most talented and innovative person in IR/PR that I have ever had the pleasure to work with, and I've worked with them all! Her ethical standards are beyond reproach."
— *Lindsay A. Rosenwald, MD, CEO, Portfolio Manager, Biotech Entrepreneur*

"Experience cannot be bought -- so thanks go to Dian Griesel for sharing her knowledge with the business community. This book provides readers with her years of experience and consequently lights the path to success."
— *Sunny J. Barkats, Esq., Partner, JS Barkats, Attorneys at Law*

"Dian tells it like it is—her 20+ years of public relations experience have given her superb insight on how entrepreneurial companies can achieve success."
— *Jon Merriman, Chief Executive Officer & Co-Chairman, Merriman Holdings, Inc.*

"Here is a book that gives company executives invaluable insight. Dian Griesel can do this because she has personally invested the time to attend the meetings she has scheduled and solicited feedback afterward. This is how I met Dian and why—10 years later—I always take meetings with her clients."

—*Leigh S. Curry, General Partner, Curry Partners*

"Executives will reap extensive rewards from Dian's two decades of corporate communications experience. Here she shares her unique perspectives on how to overcome the hurdles faced by emerging-growth companies on the road to greater success."

—*Reid Drescher, President, Spencer Clarke LLC*

"What does it take for a company to succeed in the media today? Dian Griesel knows, and in these pages she offers advice that is extremely helpful, practical and right on target. Her vigorous, honest handbooks are not to be missed."

—*Kristin L. Okesson, Market Manager, Connoisseur Media, STAR 99.9, WPLX 99.1, WFOX 95.9*

"Dian's clients have been rewarded by her invaluable out-of-the-box thinking. Her experience with all types of challenges has allowed her clients to better position their messaging. Dian's professionalism and crisis management communication skills have allowed her to provide critical and timely advice to issuers."

—*Richard H. Kreger, Managing Director and Co-Founder, Source Capital*

"FUNDaMentals is Dian Griesel at her finest. Small-cap management teams serially struggle to communicate effectively with the Street. Similar to the advice Dian provides to clients daily through her leading communications firm, FUNDaMentals provides a framework for companies to begin communicating better immediately. This book fills a big void, and is a must-read for small-cap officers and directors."

—*Adam J. Epstein, Founding Principal, Third Creek Advisors, LLC, and author of The Perfect Corporate Board: A Handbook for Mastering the Unique Challenges of Small-Cap Companies (New York: McGraw-Hill, 2012)*

"For small companies, a thorough familiarity with public relations makes all the difference between being orphaned on Wall Street or being covered. If you want the latter, you should read her books."

—*Steven Dresner, Founder & CEO, DealFlow Media/DealFlow Analytics*

"Dian Griesel has mastered the formula for reaching your company's audience. The foundation of this formula, based on thousands of one-on-one meetings, is her deep understanding of that audience and the often counterintuitive ways they think and act. The result is a clear road map to discovering your true message; to selecting the best communications tools; and to real success in conveying your message to the investment and media communities. Her books are a must-have for any business leader."

—*John J. Reed, General Partner, Azalea Ventures*

"I have known Dian for over 15 years and am constantly amazed at her creativity, talent and knack for honing the right message for growth companies to access the investment and media communities. Her books should be required reading for every business school graduate."

—*Louis Rabman, Managing Director, Conative Capital Management, LLC*

"Dian is a true professional and really understands the needs of companies in today's complex and ever-changing environment."

—*Dave Horin, CPA, President, Chord Advisors, LLC*

"Dian Griesel gives fabulous advice on how to build and run a public company plus get it media exposure. Her books help company leaders—whether new to being public or grizzled veterans—navigate dealing with investors, PR and the new world of social media. A must-read!"

—*David Feldman, Partner, Richardson & Patel and author of Reverse Mergers*

"Dian Griesel is one of the most financially savvy investor relations and public relations advisors on Wall Street. She has advised dozens of CEOs and management teams in cutting-edge technology and healthcare industries for years in relation to capital markets and public relations. I truly believe she has an understanding of what makes a good growth business and what works. Dian has built a successful career and knows from experience how to build a company from scratch. I would highly recommend her for anything. Dian is a self-made entrepreneur and has a drive and passion for what she does."

—*John Carter Lipman, Managing Director, Investment Banking, Craig-Hallum Capital Group LLC*

"A thorough familiarity with the dos and don'ts of corporate relations can make all the difference between failure and success. If you want the latter, read Dian's books."

—*Josh Scheinfeld, Managing Member, Lincoln Park Capital, LLC*

"I have worked with many IR/PR people during the course of my career, and Dian Griesel is one of the brightest and most talented. She understands her primary duty: to represent her client companies effectively. At the same time, she understands her responsibility to the financial community: to represent the right companies. Her standards are solid gold. She's got a wealth of experience that few can compare to, and tells it like it is."

—*Carl Dilley, President, Island Stock Transfer*

"From her extensive and wildly successful career as a nationwide public relations leader, Dian Griesel brings authentic, simple yet brilliant guidance to CEOs once again. Her books unlock the mysteries of attracting the media and investors like nothing I've seen in my many years doing deals for public companies."

—*Andrea Cataneo, Esq., Corporate and Securities Partner, Sichenzia Ross Friedman Ference, LLP*

"This book is the perfect guide for anybody responsible for communicating with the Street or the media. In a period when the disintermediation of capital markets is in overdrive, Dian's advice and guidance are invaluable tools to have in the toolbox."

—*J. Kevin Moran, Vice Admiral, USN, Retired*

"The most comprehensive guidance on how to grow your public company successfully and establish solid relationships with investment and media professionals. Dian Griesel is spot on."

—*Gregg E. Jaclin, Esq., Szaferman Lakind Blumstein & Blader, P.C.*

"Dian's 20+ years of public relations experience have given her unique insight on how to avoid the roadblocks that keep many emerging growth companies from ultimate success. Executives will benefit greatly from her wisdom."

—*Steven G. Martin, Managing Member, Aspire Capital Partners, LLC*

ENGAGE

Smart Ideas to Get More Media Coverage, Build Your Influence and Grow Your Business

DIAN GRIESEL, Ph.D.

A Companion Guide to the Book
FUNDaMentals: The Corporate Guide to Cultivating Investor Mindshare

THE BUSINESS SCHOOL OF HAPPINESS
CONNECTICUT

For information contact:
Business School of Happiness, Inc.
Attn: Permissions Dept.
P.O. Box 302
Washington Depot, CT 06794
860.619.0177

212.825.3210

Substantial discounts on bulk quantities are available to corporations, professional associations and other organizations. For details and discount information, contact our special sales department.

Published by Business School of Happiness, Inc.

Printed and bound in the United States of America

Line editing by Sebastian Thaler

Cover design and layout by Carla Rood Pratico

Photo: Jan Goldstoff

ISBN # 978-1-936705-13-9

Dedication

This book is dedicated to all the entrepreneurs, presidents,
CEOs and founders who have entrusted my team and me
to counsel them on the communication of their vision and mission.
Thank you for this great privilege.

Table of Contents

Note from the Author

If properly positioned, anyone and anything can attract media coverage. I know this from deep, far and wide personal experience—much of which has been publicly profiled and can be found on the Internet.

In this book, I share with you all the public relations "secrets" I have amassed over my entrepreneurial lifetime career. When applied to any person, project or company, the smart ideas within these pages will result in as much media coverage as you desire—assuming you are willing to put forth a good degree of consistent effort. The clients represented by my company further confirm this fact. We've better positioned leaders and companies in biotech, pharmaceutical, medical device, technology, national defense, consumer products, services, luxury goods, natural resources, financial services, infrastructure, ecological, wellness & beauty and countess other industries. The strategies within these pages, when joined with creativity, implementation and follow-through, result in massive news media coverage that delivers greater awareness, sales, partnerships and general interest for your company, management, product or service.

Media can help position you as a thought leader and as the "go-to" industry expert for commentary, regardless of the industry sector or the size of the other players. My company has used each of these ideas many times over for our clients, to compete against industry giants for media attention, whether print, online or broadcast. Our resulting media hits are remarkable and rival those of any large agency, which begins to explain why 100 percent of my company's business growth has resulted from word-of-mouth referrals since I began this journey more than 20 years ago.

The initial result of following this plan is that all of your relevant "publics" will see you in the media. The subsequent result is that you will be differentiated and rise into national awareness above the crowding by industry peers and the crushing by sector behemoths.

You can do all of this yourself…or you can call me.

Introduction

Engage shares 226 "smart ideas" that you can use to capture the attention of your target audiences, build influence as you establish your expert status and, as a result, power up the growth of your business to the level you seek, through lots of free media coverage.

It is a comprehensive, idea-by-idea guide that conveys exactly how to create engaging, multichannel public relations and marketing strategies. The collective of these ideas will result in maximum awareness, ongoing media coverage and online conversation about your company, project, service or self.

If acted upon, the smart ideas within these pages will help you move closer to your goal: capturing the attention of coveted customers, quality partners, fabulous potential employees and enthusiastic new investors, while inspiring them to reach out and contact you.

By explaining how to use the best of traditional media tactics in addition to social media, each page of *Engage* delivers ideas and information in a ready-to-act-upon format. As you read, you can begin testing each easy-to-implement idea to create more sales, partnerships, happy customers, great relationships and an enhanced reputation. Ultimately, you will take charge of changing perceptions and claim your position as the innovative management team and company that you are.

"Engage" is the action verb of all action verbs. It's the big daddy of verbs. It's what separates all the men verbs from the boy verbs.

You can do all kinds of things to try and grow your business. You can develop proposals and an elaborate brochure, and create cool PowerPoint presentations. You can spend a lot of money on expensively designed and clever advertisements. You can cold call a potential client. That's all well and good. But the real goal is to engage. You have not succeeded until your efforts engage with current and potential customers, vendors, partners, associates, employees, the media, investors or anyone else who might help build your business in the process.

You can converse, propose, speak, show, present, sing, dance, whatever...fill in the blank. But if you don't engage, what's it all good for? You're just another noise in a distraction-filled world, taking up someone's time while they politely (or not) wait for you to finish so they can get away and take their business elsewhere.

Imagine if you could engage as a result of each and every interaction you have, whether in person, print or broadcast. What if you could learn to use traditional print and broadcast media, new media, social media and email to accomplish your goals? Is there anything more powerful? Think about it: to acknowledge to a presenter that you were engaged is the biggest compliment you can pay. In many senses, it is the ultimate way to start a real conversation: "You engaged me. I wasn't just listening. I was fascinated. You made me think. You weren't wasting my time. This was very valuable."

Engaging your audience is not the same as getting your message heard. Engaging means that you've elicited some kind of response—whether attracting a new investor in your company or inspiring someone to take the next step toward inquiring about the product, service, technology or drug you've developed and/or want to sell.

Engage shares the smart ideas that will help you "engage" with writers, reporters and producers at coveted newspapers and magazines, television and cable shows, radio programs and Internet sites, along with the readers, listeners and viewers of these outlets. The content is relevant for corporate presidents, CEOs, CFOs, COOs, CIOs and communications officers, along with just about anybody else who desires to raise their profile or that of their company, project or concept. The book is broken down into "idea-blocks." These ultimately form the foundation for maintaining the highest-quality relationships with the media-at-large as well as your current and potential clients, partners, employees, investors, vendors, trade regulators and, for public companies, the Securities and Exchange Commission's regulatory bodies. These are the audiences that constitute the bedrock "publics" in your "relations."

For various reasons, corporate credibility with the press and public is challenged daily. Competition is fiercer than ever and technology is constantly altering the business landscape.

This new business environment demands that every corporate officer become better skilled at public relations or, at the very least, surround themselves with accomplished experts with talent and entirely new skill sets. Your ability to know what to say and when to say it—to communicate effectively to all of your public constituents, within the context of inflation or recession, volatile public markets, financial scandals, corporate missteps, worldwide terrorism and other local, national and world circumstances—is a measure of your leadership expertise and competence.

In economic downturns, as well as booms, a well-conceived corporate communications program will keep you in front of all your constituents as a winner, top brand, worthy investment, stellar product or recognizable service. Whether you are heading up a public or private company, a fund, a bank or any other kind of business or service—if you have a well-crafted communications program in action, your target investor audiences will see you as a more stable bastion for their investment dollars within your sector, as well as in the overall marketplace.

Yes, your demanding duties have increased exponentially under a variety of heightened regulatory requirements, with an increasingly litigious shareholder and activist environment added to the mix. Consequently, your imperative—as the chairman, president, CEO, CFO, COO, CIO or IRO—is to chronicle your company's progress and relay your strategic vision by delivering the good news, and if necessary the bad news, in the most transparently honest and forthright way.

Budgeting both time and money for public relations is always an interesting topic of discussion. When the economy is booming and/or stock prices are up, some management teams feel that public relations expenditures are unnecessary. Likewise on the flip side, when economic forces take a turn for the worse and operating budgets need to be tweaked, shortsighted management teams sometimes make hasty budget-cutting decisions, with their public-relations budgets the first to go.

Sophisticated management teams know the corporate communications budget is one of the *last* investments that should ever be cut. Smart managers realize the value of being in the news. They allocate a portion of their time and budget to PR because it is a wise way to continuously "accentuate the positive" and stay in the public eye.

Public relations programs don't have to be on the expense side of the corporate balance sheet. In reality, if done correctly, PR is an asset that becomes one of your best "salespeople." Done smart, communications can be designed to fit any budget, while delivering multiple returns for every dollar invested. Even better, as you will learn in these pages, much of what you can do PR-wise is free—if you know what and how to do it. Usually what you pay for is someone who knows how to be creative and how to execute.

The comprehensive ideas in this book cover the important aspects of creating and maintaining a superior public relations campaign. The sage, time-tested and up-to-the-printing-minute topics include:

- ❖ The role of good media relations in restoring investor confidence.
- ❖ Winning your case in the court of public opinion.
- ❖ Why PR is more powerful than advertising, and how you can get it for free.
- ❖ How PR can actually help lead your company to a turnaround.
- ❖ Tactics that help earn you the attention of editors and producers.
- ❖ Strategic messaging that will help you accomplish your goals.
- ❖ Proven techniques for repositioning products, brands and companies.
- ❖ How the internet is your greatest ally—and worst enemy if ignored.
- ❖ What social media is and how to use it to your ultimate advantage.
- ❖ Getting coverage in top national newspapers, magazines, TV, cable and radio.
- ❖ Creating messages and pitches that editors and producers can't ignore.
- ❖ How to position yourself as an industry expert or spokesperson.
- ❖ How to control media interviews—and why you *must*.
- ❖ Announcing bad news intelligently so that it does the least damage.
- ❖ How to respond to and recover from a scandal.

…and much, much more.

All the ideas in these pages have proven their effectiveness when used consistently as outlined. Follow them and your company will attract substantially more, and better, media placements. You and your team will be better equipped with multiple strategies for coping with crises, and have at hand the necessary tools for measuring the effectiveness of the consultants you hire to deliver messages on your behalf. You'll also learn "inside secrets" for creating the kinds of messages that move people—your publics—to respond favorably.

After you have finished reading this book, if you like what you read, but lack the time, manpower or experience to execute on each of these tactics yourself, call me. My team and I would love to help execute your corporate communications programs. At Dian Griesel International we practice what we preach and have volumes of print, radio, TV and Internet hits to document our consistently extraordinary results for companies, products and people at all stages of growth.

Enjoy the journey!

PART 1

Traditional Fundamentals for Public Relations Success

In Part I, we review the smart ideas for obtaining the best possible media coverage through the traditional outlets of newspapers, magazines and radio as well as television and cable.

CHAPTER 1:

What It Takes to Attract Favorable Media Attention Today

The rules of doing business have become more complex and sophisticated. The pitfalls and bumps in the road that companies have always encountered are no longer shallow; they have deepened into black holes that can derail a company unless it proceeds with great caution. The media and the public are, understandably, more skeptical than ever and holding up a magnifying glass to discover possible ulterior motives or "hidden truths."

There are more activists than ever who are vocal in their opposition to company expansions, projects and actions, or otherwise. These public opponents might or might not have all the facts, but there is no doubt that their misunderstandings can be shared quickly and spread. The smart ideas here will focus on how you can avoid these pitfalls and position your company as trustworthy. This chapter emphasizes the importance of honesty and commitment.

Motivational speaker Stephen Covey, in his bestseller *The Seven Habits of Highly Effective People*, said that in order to be highly effective one must:

1. Be proactive.
2. Begin with the end in mind.
3. Put first things first.
4. Think win-win.
5. Seek first to understand...then to be understood.
6. Synergize.
7. Sharpen the saw.

This is excellent advice that is completely in line with the suggestions you will find in these pages. I especially recommend you keep Covey's habit number five in mind as you read on.

SMART IDEA: Requirements for success in today's environment are pure and simple: deliver more information in a timelier manner, and make it candid, with no surprises.

Shareholders worldwide are rocked when fiduciary breaches are uncovered. The resulting damage is often uncontainable as these issues are put on public display via traditional media and the Internet. Incidents of nondisclosure and poor corporate governance can wipe out trillions of dollars of market value almost overnight.

In case you are wondering about the fallout effects of all this, let me make it clear:

1. Every publicly traded company, regardless of sector, is adversely affected each time there is a financial debacle, and

2. Every sensible investor subsequently becomes more cautious, rightly questioning every public statement made by corporate management at every public company.

The *good* news is that companies that institute good governance and high-quality communications practices will be able to create superior corporate value. This is *especially* true in skeptical climates. Today it is absolutely mandatory to be open and accountable to shareholders about what is happening in the boardroom and the company overall.

Break this rule and be prepared to suffer righteous shareholder *and* media vengeance.

SMART IDEA: Build trust and you will see progress. If you don't, you will lose.

Being forthright and direct is priceless.

Certain issues faced by corporate management might involve confronting heated public emotions. These issues generally revolve around:

- ❖ the health and safety of the population-at-large
- ❖ children
- ❖ the concerns of any large socioeconomic group
- ❖ property values
- ❖ quality-of-life issues such as freedom from fear, peace of mind and freedom from conflict

All of the above are likely to generate emotional debate. If your company is working in an area that involves any sensitive issues such as these, remember that the best defense is a good offense. Don't wait for problems to arise. Be prepared.

Management must ask the questions, anticipate and preempt criticisms and competitive points of view, and constantly address the core value concerns of the community.

This is universal. Whatever the language, the culture or the country, your company's relationship with the public must always be based on trust, forthrightness and open dialogue.

SMART IDEA: Public sentiment has tumbled more than one company. Understand the activist issues before entering the court of public opinion.

Small groups of people, even vocal individuals, can stop big companies, projects and ideas. Thanks to the Internet, it is especially easy for anyone to get an opinion out quickly. Activists stake their claims on any and all kinds of issues. More constituents are asking more questions about anything and everything. Public debates can escalate and bring out strong emotions, including embarrassment, humiliation and blame.

Public involvement, however, is often necessary, or even government-mandated. With regard to major public projects or facilities, public consent is likely to be required initially, and even continuously, throughout the planning period.

Complex scientific information about risk and probability, even when openly communicated, often results in public concern. Extensive public involvement can kill projects, companies and reputations. Smart companies take the time and trouble to translate potential issues into clear, everyday language.

A wise policy is to pay attention to public sentiment *before* a controversy draws the media. The media can be expected to focus their editorial content on the conflicts, controversy and opposition, not on your high-minded aspirations.

SMART IDEA: The current climate has spawned a new breed of activists and corporate "enemies." You don't have to be wrong to be attacked. Stay vigilant and aware of who those adversaries are, or who they might be.

Misinformation arises out of emotional responses. Activists of all kinds can and often do distort the facts in an attempt to create a grass-roots uprising. The role of public relations today includes *anticipating* resistance.

When addressing a controversial issue within your community—i.e., your company or sector—strive for peace at all times, knowing that enemies and all sorts of critics will build their forces against you, regardless. Expect them. Expect them to put endless energy into trying to derail you from moving toward your goals.

To build the trust of your community, you must:

❖ Stay in touch with your immediate community and the issues-at-large.

❖ Speak simply to your community. Don't overwhelm them with scientific or technical jargon.

❖ Provide information in advance of the questions.

❖ Ask for community input before it is asked of you.

❖ Really listen to your critics.

❖ Prove you have listened by responding and changing when practical to do so.

SMART IDEA: To build public consent, be prepared to provide 24-hour, seven-days-a-week, 365-days-a-year levels of energy and commitment to your project.

This quote is attributed to Abraham Lincoln: "You may fool all of the people some of the time; you can even fool some of the people all of the time, but you cannot fool all of the people all of the time."

If you want to introduce any potentially controversial thought, product, company, app, therapeutic, building, etc., here are a few ideas to help you build a foundation of public consent:

❖ Keep your focus on what is truly important.

❖ Consistently present your positive objectives.

❖ Have ready responses to criticisms and negative objections.

❖ Use direct communication with your investors and others in your community as much as possible, minimizing the need to go to the media, thereby reducing their potential contrarian influence.

❖ Be prepared to correct and clarify any misinformation that comes your way. Inaccurate literature or statements from antagonists and critics must be addressed rapidly to prevent miscommunication.

SMART IDEA: You might have to fight a battle more than once to win it.

Margaret Thatcher made the statement above, and I made it into a smart idea because I think it's important to keep in mind when you are considering any public relations initiative.

If you are waging a battle in the court of public opinion—which is what you are doing every time you put out a news release or attempt to influence the media in any way—think carefully about what you say. And keep in mind that you will probably have to say it more than once in order to get noticed.

I always joke with CEOs who have been plugging along for years to make their companies or projects successful that if they keep delivering, and utilize a well-orchestrated corporate communications program, some-day they, too, will be viewed as an "overnight success." Nobody will ask about the dues they paid or the many trials they suffered through to get to the pinnacle. If you don't expect credit, you won't be disappointed. Of course, you will be pleased when all the hard work you did to get where you got is appreciated.

Instead of seeking appreciation, however, focus on the greatness of the moment, of each milestone. And to position yourself for long-term success, not just your "15 minutes of fame," do everything in your power to keep all the balls rolling forward with positive momentum. This, of course, includes having a great public relations outreach program in place.

SMART IDEA: Business strategy missteps, not unrelated crises or accounting fiascos, are still the primary drivers of decline in shareholder value.

Brand marketing, brand equity and brand prominence drive shareholder value. A company's business strategy mistakes not only make the news but are the primary cause of downgrading its image in the eyes of shareholders.

The top three reasons for decline in shareholder value are:

1. Management loses touch with the marketplace.
2. Management fails to have a strong business strategy.
3. Management neglects to leverage brand assets.

Companies sometimes lose sight of the market for their products. If companies are going to rebuild what has been lost, they will need to recognize the relevance of certain basic marketing lessons. These are lessons that form the core of any sound branding strategy.

Branding value begins with:

- ❖ Knowing that loyalty is earned.
- ❖ Staying in touch with the marketplace and delivering value to customers.
- ❖ Understanding what drives product/brand demand and customer loyalty.
- ❖ Acquiring new customers and, even more critical, maintaining relationships with existing customers.
- ❖ Developing and sustaining a strong competitive position that will allow you to compete on differentiation—the things that make you unique—and thus avoid the pitfalls of downward price adjustments and pressure.

SMART IDEA: The media loves an underdog.

If David were slinging rocks at Goliath today, be assured that David would get the more favorable media coverage.

The media do indeed love the underdog. If an underdog is taking your company to task for any perceived indiscretion, people will identify with them, and they are going to be the lucky recipient of more favorable press than you.

Charges of abuse or failure to do the right thing, for example, make better stories than your denials—as accurate as those denials might be. Expect the oppositional story to see print. And if any retraction is ultimately necessary due to faulty initial reporting, expect it to appear in the classified section or some other obscure back page, in contrast to the prominence the initial accusatory story enjoyed. The solution here is to do everything you can to prevent such stories in the first place—unless of course you have your own "David" angle to exploit—by following these smart ideas to engage.

SMART IDEA: Public relations can help you be your own "turnaround specialist."

If your company is struggling through a near-death experience, public relations can help. A few years ago, Joann Lubin of the *The Wall Street Journal* interviewed Robert S. "Steve" Miller, Jr., the lead negotiator in Chrysler's loan bailout. Miller subsequently led the turnarounds of several other companies. Miller's advice, which can be readily adopted to create a successful public relations campaign during a crisis, falls largely into these three areas:

1. Tell the truth. Your personal credibility is key. Good or bad, tell it like it is, and tell anyone with the right to know—including your Board of Directors, stockholders, customers and employees.
2. Act. Do something. Don't just "study the situation" eternally. The things that need to be done are usually pretty obvious.

3. Listen to your people. Hire good public relations advisors and listen to their suggestions carefully. Give them access to your staff as necessary. Too often, management makes the mistake of becoming insulated and loses sight of what is really happening.

You can never communicate with your publics enough—IF you are doing it correctly.

SMART IDEA: Newspaper boards can be priceless allies. Smart CEOs make friends with their local newspaper's key personnel *before* there is a pressing need.

Most newspapers have editorial boards that consist of the papers' top executives. The purpose of the editorial board is to meet and assess what position the paper should take in its editorial direction. Typically, the team consists of the publisher, editor, managing editor, editorial page editor and reporters.

You need to know editorial boards:

❖ If you want to get support for a cause or issue concerning your company.

❖ When you have news pending that you want to offer on an "embargoed" basis. This could be highly sensitive news, about which you might wish to have an "off the record" conversation to enhance the perception of your position and your favorable media coverage.

❖ If you want an opportunity to present "your side" of a story— although, to be realistic, understand that they probably won't change their position.

❖ If you feel that a reporter might "have it out" for you or your company, and that you are not getting, or might not get, fair coverage.

❖ If you are a new CEO and your local paper covers local business news.

SMART IDEA: Blogger is just another name for "reporter."

Although we will delve in depth into using the Internet for better public relations in Part II, let's briefly address blogs.

In 2004, "blog" was named "word of the year" by Webster's dictionary. A blog is defined as follows:

blog *noun*: an online diary; a personal chronological log of thoughts published on a Web page; also called Weblog,

Web log. Typically updated daily, blogs often reflect the personality of the author. blog, blogged, blogging *v*, blogger *n*

Source: Webster's New Millennium™ Dictionary of English, Preview Edition (v 0.9.5) Copyright © 2003, 2004 Lexico Publishing Group, LLC

Blogging has risen to an all-time high level of popularity. A single post on a well-read blog might be echoed and expanded upon in thousands of other blogs until the chatter hits such a point that a major news agency will acknowledge the story.

Don't underestimate the power of bloggers.

Some bloggers are working very hard to build careers as reporters. Some are becoming very good reporters. They pick their topics and do their homework. Many are seeking to become well-followed, respected journalists—just like their counterparts at the well-known trades, newspapers and other traditional outlets. Accord the same respect to bloggers that you would to any other professional—or person, for that matter.

SMART IDEA: Take time to hire the right public relations firm. Or read this book carefully and use it as your definitive guidebook, along with its companion book, *FUNDaMentals: The Corporate Guide to Cultivating Investor Mindshare*, which offers advice on intelligent investor relations strategies.

Do thorough research before hiring a public relations or investor relations firm. This is essential. Poor selections are expensive and disappointing mistakes.

Put thought into what you want and can expect from your communications campaign. For example:

- ❖ Are you seeking greater exposure for your company or products?
- ❖ Are you currently a news-driven company, or is significant news a long way off in the future?
- ❖ Would your company benefit from trade media placements?
- ❖ Is your corporate spokesperson ready for national and local print and broadcast interviews, or will you need an agency that provides media coaching and rehearsal time?

If you take the time to identify your goals, you will find it easier to match your needs with the appropriate firm.

Meet the team assigned to your account. Probe the account executives at the public relations and/or investor relations firms you consider. Find out about their client-to-account executive ratio, track their success record, find out which companies like yours the agency has represented, and how the agency intends to put a dollar value on work delivered for you.

Request references, starting dates and the average length of their client/agency relationship, along with performance accomplishments during the relationship. Ask how the agency will dollarize. A good program should be measurable in several different areas:

1. increased media coverage with significance measured by either readership/reach volume or prestige of the publication
2. consistency of message and placements
3. well-written and/or ghostwritten thought-leader pieces
4. increased partnership and or sales opportunities

And possibly…

5. trading volume
6. increased institutional ownership

7. new research coverage
8. invitations to be a trade/sector conference presenter

Ask how often you'll get updates or converse with your assigned team. Although the industry standard is typically *semi-annual* progress reports, I think this is unacceptable. Weekly or semi-weekly calls are essential in addition to weekly wrap-ups of work accomplished and outstanding issues, at minimum.

Do your homework, hire the best agency you can afford and expect nothing shy of excellence.

CHAPTER 2:

Building & Sustaining Great Word of Mouth

"Good word of mouth" means people are saying good things about you. Your repuration is intact.

As these smart ideas make clear, achieving good word of mouth doesn't happen overnight, nor is it automatic. It takes work. We're talking about basic building blocks. Every brick of the foundation and building of a company must be based on strong communication to all of your public constituents including your friends and family, shareholders, analysts, investment bankers, industry and financial regulators, clients, potential partners, the media and anyone else who might be interested in your company. Follow the smart ideas in this chapter and grow your reputation for quality in your field.

SMART IDEA: A good public relations campaign requires commitment and perseverance toward pre-established goals.

It takes time to build a company—and even longer to build a brand or corporate reputation. You must be prepared to spend years doing good, hard work.

The key to success is to never give up. If you understand that it can take years to build a good public image, you will be well on your way to success. You must commit to what you are selling and believe in it. It is impossible to sell anything if you don't believe in it and are not willing to back up that belief with your time, effort and passion.

Gaining good editorial exposure also calls for a significant investment of time and effort. In terms of media coverage, to spread the news of your corporate accomplishments effectively, you need to develop targeted media lists, make press contacts, test various avenues of publicity, and do all the miscellaneous projects that go into assuring that your company is well-positioned for the long haul.

Implementing a public relations marketing campaign on an occasional basis will not work. To do so will lead to failure, as you get caught up in one trendy idea after another. This is not the way to build your image or your business. Consistency is key, as is having a focused media plan of action. That plan is essential to your success, and it must include a clear picture of the image you want your company to present to the public.

Set your goals, stick to them, and keep pushing forward with your long-term view. Public relations is the means, not the end.

If you have enough on your plate running the day-to-day aspects of your business, managing and building it, and don't also want to manage the public relations initiative that will spread the word of your ongoing successes, you are going to have to hire people internally or externally who can help you increase media awareness and attract positive coverage.

These pages will help you determine how to find an experienced PR partner who can consistently tell your story the right way to the right people.

SMART IDEA: Give your customers more than they expect.

Good public relations means managing expectations. If you keep promising more than you can deliver, you are positioning yourself for a constant struggle with the expectations of your audience, whether these are customers, investors, the media or all of the above.

Providing milestones is a good marketing tool. These provide your listening—and "buying"—audience with a tangible way to chart your progress. Make sure those milestones are realistic and, therefore, achievable.

Satisfied customers—in every category of "customer"—are repeat buyers. Customers—which include investors, the media, partners and more—are integral to the success of your public relations campaign as they become your best "free" advertisements. When you create satisfied customers, you also create walking, talking billboards for your company's products or services, and for its reputation and brand leadership.

Word of mouth is the most powerful means of advertising and of influencing positive public relations. A satisfied audience also tends to result in positive rewards financially.

SMART IDEA: Create customers with every single public relations strategy.

Every time you undertake a public relations initiative, remember that the goal is to "sell" something—your product, idea, service or shares of stock to investors. Sell you must and no one else can do that for you. It is your responsibility to let people know about your product, idea or service, and it is your responsibility to tell them where they can buy or obtain these. At best, others only provide channels. Motivation will always be up to you. And by "you," I mean you and your people, who hopefully have internalized your brand.

When we were an agricultural society, farmers brought their crops to market. Marketing, to reduce it to its essence, is bringing your company and its products or services to market. The end goal of all marketing programs, which encompass public relations and any advertising or other marketing you do, should be to create a *relationship* with each customer, not just make a sale. Satisfied customers are repeat buyers or users of whatever you offer. In designing your marketing campaign, do whatever you have to do to keep your customers happy. Specifically, in the area of public relations, a good PR campaign should never lose sight of the fact that customer service is part and parcel of your daily operating philosophy and your way of doing business.

SMART IDEA: When your competitors merge, spend more time and dollars on public relations.

In the book *Capitalize on Merger Chaos* (The Free Press, 2000), authors Thomas M. Grubb and Robert B. Lamb point out that the merging of two of your competitors could be the *best* thing to happen to your company.

From a public relations standpoint in particular, I wholeheartedly agree.

Their merger gives you at least two specific opportunities:
1. The opportunity to become a magnet for their employees, who might be tossed around in the chaos of the merger.
2. The opportunity to take advantage of their lack of external business focus.

During mergers, managers tend to be focused on business integration issues rather than current and new clients. Aggressive moves with an enhanced PR campaign might make their existing business clients or customers turn in your direction.

A third advantage I believe you might find in this situation is that the opportunity to become an expert arises. If you position yourself well, you could have the ability to comment on the viability of the merger. Even if you do not know any of the intimate details of the transaction, when stories about your sector are making the news, you want your company in there as well. This is a platinum "trend-based" story opportunity, and you can make it work for you!

SMART IDEA: The best public relations campaigns begin, and expand, through happy employees.

In *Think Like a Champion: Building Success One Victory at a Time* (Harper Business Press, 2000), Denver Broncos coach Mike Shanahan shares his insight into the principles of creating a winning team on—or *in*—any field.

His 15-point game plan for winning teams is as follows:

1. Teams matter more than individuals.
2. Every job is important.
3. Treat everyone with respect.
4. Share both victories and defeats.
5. Accept criticism.
6. Keep the boss well-informed.
7. Focus on your work ethic, not others.
8. Allow for differences in lifestyle.
9. Be more creative than predictable.
10. Let go of failed ideas.
11. Employ structure and order.
12. Reward those who produce.
13. Find different ways to motivate your employees.
14. Keep your employees fresh.
15. Protect your system.

Not much more I can add to this simple, wise list!

CHAPTER 3:

How to Develop Solid, Lasting Media Contacts

You might already have PR strategies in place, or you might just be starting out. Either way, you should know that the name of the game is *contacts*: identifying the media outlets to target and uncovering which reporters, editors and producers to pitch. How do you find them? As you will see, they are often right there, hidden in plain sight. Follow the smart ideas in this chapter and they will help you build your roster of media contacts.

SMART IDEA: Read all the appropriate trade and consumer magazines.

To ensure that your public relations placements are being or will be noticed by the appropriate audience, start subscribing to and reading all appropriate industry, trade and consumer publications. Identifying your target of industry-related publications will lead you to the right reporters, editors and producers. In addition to reading trade magazines and newsletters, also visit the relevant industry websites. All of this research can help you better understand distribution issues, develop your perspective as to what retailers are looking for, see what new trends are getting coverage, learn how to attract advertising to your market and gain other valuable "insider" information.

Read consumer magazines to:

❖ Assess their editorial content for suitability to your objectives

❖ Get a better picture of advertisers and the angles they use to reach their market; often, these are the advertisements of your competitors—so you can get "inside" the competition a bit

❖ Assess the messages that the editorial pages of these publications deem worthy of dissemination to their audiences.

Note which kinds of topics, angles and trends are getting the most coverage, what subjects are regularly referred to in columns and what the readers' concerns are. For example, are there "Question and Answer" columns you could contribute to? (Yes, these are usually scripted, believe it or not!) Do they have "Issues and Solutions" articles? Can you become one of the experts discussing these challenges and offering answers?

You will increase your odds of appearing in any publication if you give its editors what they want. You will *not* get your story told if the editor or publisher feels your story will not help sell copies, subscriptions or advertising. If you can't take the time to look into the style and editorial format of each publication you desire to be within, hire someone who can do it for you. Otherwise you are wasting valuable time and losing important opportunities.

SMART IDEA: Learn what type of articles specific reporters are writing.

If you want to initiate a successful public relations campaign—and of course you do!—you and your employees and friends must gather and circulate clips of stories you see in publications that are, directly or indirectly, related to your business sector.

On any given day, my in-box contains at least 100 stories compiled by my co-workers. The stories usually apply to some aspect of public relations, financial communications, the stock market or one of our clients' sectors, businesses or products.

All of these stories can be used to your advantage—if you see them, are creative and act.

For example, let's say you see a story about one of your competitors. You immediately know that this reporter is interested in your business segment. This is a door now open wide for you to enter and an opportunity for you to initiate a conversation with that journalist!

The easiest way to initiate contact with a reporter is to say, "I read that article you wrote and thought it was (choose one or more: *thought-provoking, informative, balanced, well-written,* etc.)" After allowing the reporter to bask a moment in your sincere praise, continue with, "Considering your interest in this topic, I thought you might also like to know (explain how your business or the story you are telling fits in)…"

They might not be immediately responsive. They might say, "I'm finished with that story." That's okay—don't push, and resist telling them their story would have been better if they had included you and your company! Instead, accept that you have let them know that in the future, you are an ideal resource who can broaden their storyline. If you are really clever, and well prepared with several bullet-pointed story angles, you might just be able to convince them that there is a worthwhile follow-up story. Clever is the key word here. So I'll repeat: you never want to imply that the reporter's original story was lacking. Rather, you want to provide the reporter with angles for additional coverage on the topic, and you want to become a resource for future stories in your arena.

When you read magazines and newspapers, watch television or listen to the radio, listen and read *consciously* to find topics that can connect you with writers and editors.

Remember—writers work hard as they have to first pitch their editor on the validity of a story angle. An editor is trying to determine if the publisher—who is also overseeing the advertising department—will find the story worthy. For a story to be print or air worthy, the publisher or executive producer has to believe that the advertisers—who pay big time for their coverage—will benefit and want to be affiliated with the content. Keep the roles of all the players in mind—along with the big picture—and you will likely pass your competitors in free, coveted magazine, newspaper, radio, television, cable and Internet coverage.

SMART IDEA: Track down the right reporter.

To get a story in print, you might have to contact four, five or even more freelance or staff reporters at a newspaper before you find one who will listen to your pitch. Many times, we send information to multiple reporters and editors and follow up with them many, *many, many, many* times before we get coverage. I could add about 100 more "many"s and not be exaggerating! However, take it from me—persistence pays, royally! If you believe your story is worthy of print, keep calling until you find the right reporter or editor. Sometimes, one section of a newspaper or magazine will reject your news release, while another will enthusiastically accept it. Rejections don't mean that the publication is not appropriate for your story. It might just mean you have not yet found the right reporter.

Don't discount freelance writers. To get your story into a newspaper or magazine, it pays to track down those freelance writers who write articles—especially *frequent* articles—for the particular publication you're targeting. Look for freelancers who specialize in writing about subjects related to your company or business sector. A freelancer might like freelance status or they might be seeking a full-time reporter role. Either way, having access to creative, thoughtful experts increases those reporters' odds of another story. And just as in sales, if you're a reporter, you're only as good as the next story that will sell ads.

When you find published news or feature articles in your area of business, begin making lists of every reporter and publication covering your topics. Soon you will have accumulated a healthy media list of likely candidates. Since reporters tend to write on topics in a preferred genre—health, money, luxury goods, technology, sports, new trends, medicine, etc.—you'll be able to organize your lists to better target your pitches.

SMART IDEA: Search for and read your competitors' press releases.

Quite often, in ways that you might not have noticed, your competitors distinguish themselves through distinctive language they use in their news releases.

A smart way to unearth reporters covering your sector is to look for keywords found in your competitors' press releases. Input them into search engines and you will discover who is using their releases, which gives you another opportunity to expand on these stories.

Once you have the reporter's name and publication, you are on your way to a new contact who might be interested in highlighting you and your company in their next story.

A suggestion here: Google and Google often. Use Google's comprehensive search engine to quickly find out which reporters are covering topics like yours. Make sure you also review the other "suggested" phrases Google serves up at the bottom of the first page of your search. They are likely to trigger additional smart ideas.

SMART IDEA: Never underestimate the power of a business trade journal story versus a big-circulation newspaper story.

Business and trade journals are valuable—and sometimes *more* valuable—than a story about your company in the business section of a higher-circulation metropolitan or national newspaper. There are three main reasons.

Business trade journals:

❖ Have a shelf life of at least a week and often a month, compared to a newspaper, which stays on the stands for only 24 hours.

❖ Include stories that tend to be written with much more in-depth, insightful coverage. That is the nature of these publications and the reason their audiences buy them.

❖ Attract more high-level business people. The coverage is generally target-specific rather than "one-size-fits-all."

Business trade journals often demand the "first scoop" of a business news story, which is something you should give to them. Newspapers might even subsequently pick up the story. But unless it's a story gleaned from a business journal, or a really exciting trend-based roundup article, the front page of a big-city newspaper or a feature in the business section is often reserved for major national news or trends that concern large numbers of people.

Study the format of the trade journals you would like to have cover your company. They tend to have standard sections and columns. Knowing which these are and who writes them will make it easier to target the appropriate reporter.

Once you get coverage in a trade, be sure to put out a press release announcing it! The reason? There are many people who read trade publications. However, there are many people interested in the innovation and exciting news coming from your company who don't. By putting out a press release announcing your trade journal coverage, you are getting a double bang for the buck! By being highlighted in the trade, you received recognition—but you increase that exponentially when you tell the non-trade world you were worthy of a third-party endorsement… which is what coverage in any outlet is.

One more thing—thank the reporter. Always. Send a note. Be gracious. Remember, whenever we are talking about public relations, we are talking about relationships! I will discuss this in more detail later on.

SMART IDEA: Never underestimate the PR power of an article in an in-flight magazine.

If you want affluent, "high-flying" investors to read about the great things going on at your company, make sure you, or someone who fulfills the PR function for you, spend time targeting the glossy in-flight magazines that each airline publishes.

Statistics prove the point:

❖ On average, 57 percent of their readers earn more than $75,000 annually.

❖ 60 percent of the readers are men, 40 percent women.

❖ 74 percent of the reading travelers are in the 25 to 54 age bracket.

❖ 86 percent have a college education.

❖ 56 percent hold jobs in management.

❖ The circulation and pass-along rate is high, due to the number of passengers traveling each month—many of whom take the magazines home.

Stories that fit these publications are focused on business news, trends in food and restaurants, special events, celebrities, localities and tourist attractions. They also like profiles of interesting people who are breaking new ground.

These stories are very hard to get for free and usually fall into the pay-for-play category. But, remember, as Wayne Gretzky said, "You miss

100 percent of the shots you don't take." So keep pitching these editors and one day you might score.

SMART IDEA: Hire a clipping service—or utilize Google search religiously. Locate, clip and save all the articles about you, your company and your employees.

Proof that you or a company spokesperson has been successfully interviewed can be a big help in getting booked for a television show or written about in another newspaper or magazine.

Keep all copies of newspaper and magazine stories in which you or your company are mentioned—even small notices and announcements. Also, order duplicate recorded copies of any show featuring you or your company, as well as transcripts of any radio interviews.

Every article or appearance is evidence of how well you've done in interviews, how well one of your executives did and how newsworthy your company is.

SMART IDEA: Reach out annually to any reporter who ever covered your company in a story.

Folks with public relations savvy reach out on an annual basis to all the media people who ever highlighted their company. Since you are now becoming a media maven, you'll want to do the same.

The idea is twofold:

1. A friendly call when you're not pitching a story is a good way to keep in touch with reporters and establish a relationship. If you've got new stories for them—and you should!—let them know you've been thinking about them and about that great story they wrote earlier.

2. When you think of a good angle or angles for a follow-up story and make the call, you might be surprised—and of course pleased—to find that your call is greatly appreciated. Reporters deal with

rejection too—from their editors. They know their odds of getting an assignment improve if they can present a topic that has a history of seeing print or, even better, sparking the sale of an advertisement or two.

Again, discipline and a significant investment of time are required to create a successful public relations program. You can do these things yourself, or hire a competent firm to make sure this type of regular, effective media outreach is included in your overall marketing plan.

SMART IDEA: Make at least one new media contact each month.

The late, great advertising executive Tony Wainwright, who at one point was the CEO of Saatchi & Saatchi Advertising, personally taught me the value of letter writing and of offering free information to anyone who might be interested in it. Tony had a networking group of more than 3,000 people whom he deliberately referred to as his "friends," not as mere "contacts." Judging from the turnout at his memorial service, I'd say he was right.

Tony's approach was simple. For more than 20 years, he followed a policy of writing at least six letters a day—five to people he already knew and one to someone he *wanted* to know. The results were phenomenal. Tony made people—especially his clients—feel important because he showed them he was always thinking about them. If he saw an appropriate article in a newspaper, he clipped it and included it in his letters.

The letters were short—five lines at a maximum. Most importantly, they always ended with some sort of request. The technique prompted the reader to respond. This was also his way of building a personal public relations program.

At my company, we target a reporter every time we see an article that could even remotely apply to one of our clients. We contact them and offer them another perspective, for now or for the future. This policy has built us an incredibly deep Rolodex of media contacts, all due to a willingness to reach out, stay in touch and share ideas.

Start building your own database, one that includes personal information about the reporter whenever possible—for example, the names of his or her spouse and children, birthday, likes and dislikes, and areas of interest.

If you don't want to do this, you can always hire a quality firm. But ask if they are already putting this strategy in place and continually building on it every day.

CHAPTER 4:

Creating a Media Message That Can't Be Ignored

Your good speaking and writing skills are assets to your business. However, these skills will only serve you well if you have clearly defined your message. Before you pick up the phone to make a pitch, before you write a single word of a press release, *before you open your mouth*, you have to think carefully about what you want to say. In business, as in politics, the importance of staying "on message" is continually emphasized. This is no different in public relations. The engaging ideas in this chapter will help you find and perfect your core message.

SMART IDEA: Never put out a press release, or give a presentation at a meeting or conference, without clearly identifying the single most important message you want your audience to take away with them.

Your most important key message is simply the answer to this question: "What makes you different from your competitors?" Figure that out first, and then drive that difference home with every announcement, interview and/or comment you make. And never forget this key message in your media outreach program.

A major component of a worthwhile presentation is *targeted messaging*. What is the particular point—again, the key message—that you want any person to hear and walk away with as you speak? In terms of the media, what is the most important thing you want readers, viewers and listeners to remember about you and your company?

The goal of a public relations campaign is similar to that of an advertising campaign: to make your target consumers aware, in a positive way, of your company and what it offers—specifically, the unique benefits you offer them. The companies that are most successful are those that understand their corporate mission, and never waver from communicating these core messages in their public relations program.

Good presenters practice delivering their core message in several different ways. They also take the time to anticipate questions on a variety of subjects, and they work at giving their answers with flair. Think carefully about what your message is and deliver it succinctly. Make your point. Don't wander. Start specific and stay specific—illustrating your points if and when necessary.

If you need media training, get it. There are outstanding media coaches. Coaching is not expensive and can make a major difference in how you are perceived by the media, at industry events, at shareholder meetings, on fundraising road shows and, in fact, *anywhere* you appear to represent your company. This could be some of the best money you spend.

SMART IDEA: Honesty in your message has never been more fundamental to your success.

This point cannot be overemphasized! Honesty is *the* critical element in your public relations strategies. This is especially so for a publicly traded company since investors, consumers and the media can easily access corporate documents and financial filings on the Internet.

Companies need to be more transparent. In fact, the best-run public relations departments or external teams create a two-way flow of communications between the company and all potentially interested constituents.

Be proactive and forthright. Those are your best communication tactics. Let the media add the hype or exaggeration—the "bragging"—to your story. If you've presented your facts accurately, you'll have nothing to worry about, because even if the story ultimately runs with exaggerations or distortions, you did not put them out. And for the record: if you are heading up a public company, the media are exempt from Regulation Fair Disclosure (Reg FD). But here's a BIG caveat: make 100 percent sure you are talking with legitimate media and not some unscrupulous poser who is looking for insider information.

SMART IDEA: Keep an idea file.

For more than 20 years, I've kept a file—many files, actually—of articles, direct mailings sent to me that I really liked, good media releases, tables of contents, sales brochures I thought were creative, annual shareholder letters, and magazine and newspaper covers with clever headlines. I have often been able to extrapolate ideas, and even actual "sound bite" copy, from someone else's creative marketing genius. These have helped my company and many of the companies in our portfolio of clients.

Files like these are handy references. When I am trying to get my creative juices flowing, a review of my now-voluminous idea file is the perfect way to ignite the spark that fires up my thinking.

SMART IDEA: Find a "hook."

Don't overlook any opportunity for publicity. Read, read, *read* newspapers and magazines to assess what kinds of stories are getting traction and coverage. Watch TV and cable business shows and news segments. Listen to radio talk programs. Pay close attention. See if you can "find the hook." The "hook" is the trend, issue or news event that is attracting attention to these articles or segments. See if you can connect your company, yourself or a specific story idea to what is already happening or about to happen in your arena or in the world. When you can find a hook that relates to your company, you can more easily get it the news.

Here is a short list of the ways you can piggyback publicity from other news or events to benefit your company:

- ❖ *Anniversaries:* Practically any day is the anniversary of something. How can your company tie into that for media coverage?

- ❖ *TV Series:* Newspapers and magazines often get their story ideas from newsmagazine shows such as *20/20* and *60 Minutes*. You can do the same thing. Pay attention to what is being aired, and contact reporters to try to tie your story into whatever late-breaking news they might be using for their publications.

- ❖ *Local Interests:* When sending out press releases, make special mention of any local angles.

- ❖ *Holidays/Seasons:* We've successfully pushed products and companies that have seasonal tie-ins to the media. For example, a biotechnology company working on a diet drug is likely to get increased coverage at the start of a new year and early summer when everyone is thinking about dieting and their waistlines. And for the record, it doesn't make any difference if your drug, product or solution might not come to market for years. You're making news by tying into the discussion and sharing "what's to come."

❖ *School Season:* Pay attention to the start of school, spring break, etc. A story we syndicated more than five years ago about oral vaccines *still* gets picked up each September at the start of the school year when parents are thinking about vaccinations. The product is still under development, years from coming to market. Nonetheless, editors find it newsworthy!

❖ *Current Events:* Scan the daily newspapers for current news you might use to further publicize your company. Be on the lookout for the offbeat as well as headline news.

SMART IDEA: Use advertorials.

If you want to comment on some issue, trend or problem and the local newspaper or magazine doesn't want to print your editorial, consider buying advertising space and run your views as an advertorial instead.

You've seen what these look like. The layout is very similar to the magazine or newspaper's typical layout—using the same typestyle and formatting. But usually they have a fine line border around the copy and an italicized line identifying the content as "paid for" advertising.

Nonetheless, this kind of copy works well. It might be the way to get yourself noticed by the audience you seek.

SMART IDEA: Capitalize on weird stories.

Although nobody likes to admit it, print and online outlets that post stories about zombies rising from the dead, Elvis returning to Earth via Mars and the next Kardashian husband, get lots of readers.

Sometimes, I get my best PR ideas when reading these headlines. They spark creativity. Collect these weird stories from sources your readers don't usually see—or admit to seeing. If your audience is a group of scientists working on the next new drug to get us all skinny, connect to news stories highlighting bizarre weight loss ideas. Tie into the ridiculousness of the theories and be the voice of sanity. If someone is working on new three-dimensional ways to see into the human brain or body, share news about space exploration and the most advanced telescopes. This method of tying into news trends can be done with any topic. Sift through and find the metaphors and analogies in these stories that will relate to your topic.

Quirky, oddball stories make all content more compelling. Results happen only when your content is worth reading.

SMART IDEA: "Steal" from the best headline writers.

I confess: I get major inspiration for headlines while on line at the grocery store. The covers of the *New York Post, Woman's World, Star, Cosmopolitan* and countless other magazines capture my attention and inspire me and my staff to create killer story headlines that also jump from the page into the minds of readers.

Headline writers at these outlets are paid big bucks to get you to drop some impulse dollars on their magazines—so you pay for a bunch of information you could get for free online.

Search for your best article/content headlines from magazines that have absolutely nothing to do with your topic! Yes, seriously. This strategy will inspire your creativity. You'll be surprised by how you can tie into something quite far-fetched at first glance—if you think about it long and hard enough! Your most popular posts will originate from using this technique.

SMART IDEA: Address objections with content.

Every objection you, your company or sales staff has ever faced can be very effectively addressed using content. The content you create for articles, blogs or other promotional materials presents a unique opportunity to counter every objection you've ever faced when trying to sell your product. Write and share articles that demonstrate your product or service, and go through the objections. This approach allows you to calmly and thoughtfully counter oppositional thinking while presenting your value proposition in an organized, orderly manner.

Along these lines, do you have a client who would be willing to share an "interview" testimonial about your company, employees, services or products? You can offer this as a "test drive" to people who are thinking about working with you. Testimonials are a great sales tool. Live interviews with happy customers or partners singing your praises are even better. These are ways you can build assurances that your new partner, client, investor, employee or anyone else is aligning themselves with a worthy team.

SMART IDEA: Write an industry report on a trending hot topic.

Assembling and disseminating an industry report is a great way to raise your stature within any community. Don't worry about whether you personally have enough to say about any given topic: you don't have to be the sole author or commentator. Request that others share their opinions with you in your report. You'll be pleasantly surprised by how many high-profile people will agree to lend their views for an industry report.

Pick the topic. Create your theme. Choose a wish list of guest contributors. Reach out, edit their contributions and publish. Then publicize your report with a news release and a link to the website or blog where it is posted. Offer to book interviews for every contributor.

You will not only win friends…but you'll influence people!

SMART IDEA: Celebrity cachet and gossip outlets can make you the star.

Even if it is a stretch, whenever possible, tie a celebrity to your product. This tactic can bring out the media coverage in droves. There are many highly creative ways to do just this. Think about how a celebrity—whether the trendiest vampire actor, most accomplished athlete or hottest singer—*might* be able to use your product, service, technology, biotechnology or whatever you are offering. I italicized "might" because that celeb doesn't necessarily have to be using your product—but is there a way they might benefit from using it? Followed carefully, this rule can greatly enhance coverage. The fact is, whether people admit it or not, lots of high-net-worth investors, customers, partners, potential key employees and the media secretly read gossip headlines, columns, publications and websites!

Here's an example of the impact this smart idea can deliver. After the American Psychiatric Society (APS) added "orthorexia: an obsessive desire for health" to its dictionary, my company capitalized on this. We wrote an article that asked whether Jack LaLanne, the founder of the modern health and exercise movement, could have been orthorexic. We included a quote from the authors of the *TurboCharged*® book series—myself and my brother, even though there was no direct connection between us and LaLanne or the APS—and the story was picked up more than 1.3 million times worldwide within hours. This opportunistic approach certainly boosted general awareness of the series and book sales!

If you want media coverage, be bold. At my company, we leave no stone unturned, nor should you. And for the record, "Page Six" of the *New York Post* attracts more than one million affluent readers daily. *The National Enquirer*—which few admit to reading—actually has five million readers, many of them people who can buy your stock. By covering celebrities and trends, Perez Hilton has made himself a celebrity. His broad readership represents potential consumers, partners and investors of yours.

When creating a media action plan, one that is completely appropriate for you and your company, try to think both inside and outside the box. It is always great to get written about in *The New York Times, The Washington Post, The Wall Street Journal, Investor's Business Daily, Forbes, Fortune* and *Bloomberg BusinessWeek*—but outlets such as *AARP Bulletin, The Costco Connection,* men's and women's magazines, gossip rags and others can be the match that ignites greater awareness of your company. Don't limit your possibilities. You can always wait on a "crazy" idea— but it is always good to encourage and consider them!

SMART IDEA: The best "reader-interest" angles focus on safety, health, education, social responsibility, social trends, novelty, celebrity and general human interest.

Could you ever have imagined that a company built on fossil fuels would regularly use the *environment* as its sales and marketing pitch? ExxonMobil does.

Kenneth Cole Productions, Inc. is building an empire by tying every campaign it creates to social responsibility. Even those that initially backfired ultimately succeeded.

Las Vegas maintains its edgy, glamorous, insular-fun mystique with its "what happens here, stays here" campaign.

When you are brainstorming headlines and story angles, remember these tips:

❖ Health, diet and longevity stories help outlets sell advertisements. Consequently, they will always get news coverage.

❖ Personal issues, school and national security concern everyone.

❖ Novelty sells. Amazement abounds when someone creates a unique item such as a hula hoop. Nostalgia reigned as hula hoops were reignited as a hot exercise trend and this received plenty of free media coverage.

61

SMART IDEA: Put a face on it.

The secret to getting great coverage for your safety, education, health, social responsibility, social trend and general human interest articles is to put a face on your story. A person whose life was enhanced in any way by your company's product, service, technology or drug will attract and receive more press coverage than "dry" news on your company's product or service developments. Even a potential end-user is a possibility—namely, someone who might be looking forward to being helped by your company's offerings, and can tell a captivating story and rivet attention.

The real person whose life was made easier thanks to your company's amazing technological developments puts a relatable face on a story, and gives a reporter something to work with that becomes a "human interest" piece—versus what can otherwise seem to be an advertorial for your company.

For broad-based pickup of your company's news, assess every bit of information you release to determine whether you can better position the general angle in a way that will attract bigger and better coverage.

Media releases are designed to interest reporters in covering your story. Clear, compelling and brief releases give accurate information, do not sensationalize the news, focus on a main message, and introduce only two or three additional messages to support the main message. Having a great angle with a history of real human success stories for others is always your best strategy.

SMART IDEA: Trends and long-term issues will both get coverage—just learn to differentiate the two.

The easiest way to explain this concept is as follows:

Health concerns, particularly if weight-related, are long-term issues. People will always be concerned about their health and the numbers on the scale. This is why it is a common theme in so many news stories.

62

Many of the assorted diets people try, constitute trends: gluten-free, vegan, high-fiber, low-carb, high-protein, low-fat…the list goes on.

Trends come and go. However, if you want to get fast press coverage, it can be extremely powerful to spot and jump on a trend while it's hot.

Likewise, you want to focus on long-term, underlying issues—for example, the underlying socioeconomic causes and costs of obesity and its long-range prognosis, factoring in your company's possible role in this picture.

When the Internet arrived, countless companies began to explore how it could be used to create or improve their businesses. For example, all kinds of "social" sites popped up and tried to recruit members. MySpace, Plaxo, LinkedIn, Facebook and many others appeared. The long-term issue has become how these communities can remain viable and generate revenues. The Facebook IPO on May 18, 2012 became the largest tech offering—and third-largest overall—in U.S. history. Yet it is still to be determined whether Facebook can figure out how to stay vital with fickle audiences and earn enough in revenues to justify its valuation.

Every sector has trends and long-term issues. Study the news and see which trends and long-term issues you can capitalize on to garner greater media coverage for your company.

SMART IDEA: Your corporate "anniversaries" offer great opportunities for enhancing your PR program.

A few pages back, we touched on using anniversaries for story hooks. Holidays and significant world or historical events are the more obvious anniversary ideas. But there are two other worthy public relations angles that can be incorporated to draw press attention to your own "anniversaries."

First, there is the opportunity to create and announce your company's own holiday, one that is related to your product or service. Be bold and invent your own anniversary! Company-specific anniversaries might be focused on founding date, major product launches, expansions, entry into new geographies, new factories/buildings and key executive appointments.

Second, don't rule out the negative events in your history—a bankruptcy, for instance. Adversity, believe it or not, can provide a great opportunity to garner free press. Picture the headline: "Just two years after declaring bankruptcy, X Company has entered a new era. Today the company proudly (released, announced)…"

Everybody likes the "comeback kid," so don't overrule the positive advantages of highlighting your redemption from disaster in your anniversary-related public relations program.

SMART IDEA: The survey gets press.

A while back, I read about a survey that really caught my attention. Cintas Corp., a provider of restroom hygiene services for businesses, determined that the John Michael Kohler (of Kohler bathroom products fame) Arts Center in Sheboygan, Wisconsin has the best restrooms in America. Each of the six public washrooms in the Kohler Arts Center was created by an outstanding American artist in the Arts Center's renowned Arts/Industry program, utilizing—what a surprise!—Kohler bathroom products.

This news, which resulted from a contest that reportedly attracted more than 200 entrants from businesses, movie theaters, high schools, golf courses, museums and restaurants, helped both Kohler and Cintas get their names in print repeatedly in a wide range of publications.

Can you think of an industry trend that you can survey? Once you have one identified, conduct your survey, disseminate the results in a news release, and don't be surprised to be rewarded with lots of stories that highlight your survey results.

SMART IDEA: Testimonials serve as great third-party endorsements.

Ever since my first book was published more than 20 years ago, right through to the one you are holding in your hands, I have asked industry leaders to give each book a read prior to publishing. More boldly, I ask that if they find it worthy, would they be kind enough to contribute a brief quote to include on the cover or opening pages of the book.

Receiving these quotes has always been thrilling. They are a wonderful acknowledgment that always feels great. More importantly, though, each of these endorsements adds to the perception that I am an expert in corporate and personal public relations.

A well-written testimonial gives people confidence in your company or product. People are likely to react more favorably if others have been satisfied in their ongoing relationship with you.

How *do* you get testimonials?

First, you boldly ask for them.

Then, you look for them in your everyday life. For example, read your emails. If one contains a compliment, ask the sender if you can reuse it to your advantage and quote them.

Other strategies? Use customer satisfaction cards. Put out requests for feedback on a regular basis.

And a word to the wise: do not use anonymous testimonials. Never ever. If you can't cite a name and company or location of the person giving the testimonial, skip it. Otherwise you'll destroy your credibility instead of enhancing it. The value of a testimonial is that an identifiable person provided it. It's a form of "reality programming."

SMART IDEA: Sex and controversy sell.

You've heard it before and you'll briefly hear it here: sex sells. If you can find a seductive angle to your story, you will significantly increase the odds of penetrating the media and getting coverage.

Whether or not you like the always-controversial Madonna, 30 years after her arrival on the music scene, she still knows how to attract free press coverage. Whether via a new album, a marriage, a boyfriend, kissing Britney Spears on stage, releasing children's books or walking off stage because someone was smoking at her concert—she has mastered the sex and controversy angle in order to focus media attention on herself and her projects. Likewise, it's a good possibility you might know more than you want to about Kim Kardashian, Kanye West, Katy Perry and countless other boldfaced names as well.

Controversy and a sexy angle beget media coverage. Sexy controversy is front-page news—not that I recommend pursuing this angle unless you can do so with minimal backlash.

SMART IDEA: Whoever gets the public's attention first, wins a distinct advantage.

In situations dealing with controversy, whoever gets the public's attention first usually has the advantage of controlling the conversation and getting their points out and heard, instead of being put in a defensive position. For example, think about the advantage held by the incumbent president versus the challengers.

Public discussions are often so blasé and humdrum that the first to offer a new angle on an ongoing story is likely to get the coveted exposure. Be circumspect, of course, but also be bold.

SMART IDEA: Get mileage out of your press releases announcing executive appointments.

It is common to send out a brief media release when a company hires a new member of its management team or when someone at a company earns a major promotion. These are good for getting free publicity in "People on the Move"-type columns in the business sections of newspapers and magazines, as well as in college alumni publications and local newspapers.

If written properly, news like this carries a potential twofold benefit. First, the very act of getting your company's name in the news reminds the public of all the good things you are doing and the fact that you are an attractive employer. Secondly, it's a welcome ego boost for the company executive who gets the exposure and the public pat on the back.

If you are savvy, you can also use this type of release to generate significant publicity above and beyond the "Movers and Shakers" columns. The key to broadening your press coverage here lies in explaining *why* the move is significant to the company and perhaps to your market sector as a whole.

What reasons can you highlight in your executive hire releases that help explain your advancing business direction and excitement? The special ingredient in the release is *context*. Can your subhead relay significance? If it does, you might have entered the realm of news, rather than business as usual. Sharp business editors will see that a local company is doing something more significant than simply announcing a new hire; it's growing, expanding reach, building presence and adding new structure.

Increase the coverage by adding the "why" while offering an interview with your new executive. Lastly, don't forget to include a current photo of that person, looking his or her best, when you disseminate your release.

SMART IDEA: Stories about your competitors are golden opportunities.

Whenever you see an article or television news spot about one of your competitors, you should let out a big "Yippee!" Don't lament that you are not part of the story. Rather, consider that you now have an opportunity to contact a reporter or producer you know is interested in your industry segment and its products.

The next time you see an article about one of your competitors, seize the opportunity by tearing out the story and contacting the reporter who wrote it to tell him or her about your angle on the news.

Don't start your conversation by complaining that you weren't part of the original scoop. That won't help your case or get you more print—but might trigger a hang-up! Instead, use the story to start your conversation and build a relationship with the writer. Capitalize on the opportunity to creatively expand the story by offering your related ideas.

Compliment the writer, then offer another angle or two, and go into your full pitch.

The media love a horse race. Competition gets media attention—especially when the competitors are visibly challenging each other, issuing public statements, holding debates in public forums, willing to talk in front of cameras, and so forth.

For more coverage, think of a way you can challenge your competition. The challenge doesn't even necessarily have to name your nemesis. Remember the national advertising campaign for Avis? "We're number two, so we try harder." The company in the number one spot was marginalized as the campaign cast doubt, causing people to wonder, "Which company is working harder for my business?" Or simply, "Which company will ultimately deliver the best service?"

SMART IDEA: The "reason why" is the most important part of any public relations campaign designed to influence consumers.

I can't remember where, but I once read that…

"Free" will capture public attention,

and that…

"Because" will capture market share.

Because = Reason why.

If you want folks to pay attention, get rid of any perceptions of hype by adding the word "because."

"Because" calls for a suspension of disbelief. Suddenly, the person on the receiving end of such a statement begins to think that the claims are valid. Why? Because.

Think in these terms:

Our drink is better because…it is 100 percent fruit juice.

Our service is superior because…we care.

Our airplane is more comfortable because…we provide 180-degree reclining seats.

Our mail service is best because…we deliver the fastest.

Every time you speak with the media, find a way to remind your customers of your great brand or product, and its thoroughly believable benefits.

SMART IDEA: Reverse-engineer your stories.

Reverse-engineering a press release means starting with a story that's making headlines and finding a way to connect it to your company. There are dozens of news events happening every day that can be logically tied into your business. Don't miss those opportunities.

Help the reporters do their jobs. Tie your local angle into national stories. Help newspapers, magazines, radio and television shows sell their stories by bringing in a human-interest angle whenever possible. If you can provide the media with real news, they will be delighted to feature your company.

To develop real news, you must keep refining your news hooks until you find those that really meet others' needs. Don't send out press releases highlighting your wonderful company, hoping for coverage, unless you can show that you provide at least one benefit to potential readers or viewers—whether that benefit is entertainment, information, instruction or enlightenment.

SMART IDEA: You don't need "new" news to break a news story.

Over the past 20 years, I've been amazed how often a potential new client has made excuses for its prior agency's lack of performance by stating: "We haven't been able to deliver much news—so they really weren't able to get us any media coverage."

Let me state unequivocally: you don't need "new" news to get media coverage. But you might need a new communications agency if you're not in the news...

I've made a career and built my communications businesses by knowing how to break national news stories whether or not there is "new" news from a company.

How can you do this? It's actually easier than you might think—if you use your imagination and existing history. All you'll be doing is coming up with several angles that tell your ongoing business story in different ways. Below is a simplification of the formula we use to produce news releases about a company that actually has no "new" news:

1. Work on writing a story about your company, describing its existing business, the principals and the market it serves. Then put it out in a release.

2. Do a "hook" announcement. This is where you somehow tie your company to   some breaking news story or event.

3. Write an "industry issues and solutions" announcement.

4. Write an announcement highlighting your website and what it offers.

5. Write an educational roundup release, e.g., "The 10 Things You Can Do to…" Then prominently weave your product(s), service(s) or company into that Top 10, Top Five, the "Single Most Whatever" list, etc.

6. Send out an interview with your company president or product developer.

7. Design, initiate and publicize a survey that applies to your target market.

8. Write and offer targeted publications an article on alternative uses, perspectives or basically contra-trend thinking within your industry.

By the time you finish this whole cycle, your company will most likely have a new development that can be marketed as "new" news. Upon this event, put out a new feature or milestone announcement, and remind everyone of all the prior great coverage that folks might have read highlighting your company in the recent past.

SMART IDEA: Keep it simple.

According to author Robert Slater in *Jack Welch and the GE Way* (Mc-Graw-Hill, 1998), "Keep it simple" was the blueprint followed by Welch in transforming GE. Welch is quoted as saying: "Simple messages travel faster, simpler designs reach the market faster, and the elimination of clutter allows faster decision making."

Simplicity takes on several meanings in business. To an engineer, it means clean, functional designs with fewer parts. In manufacturing, it's judging a process by how understandable it is to those who make it work. In marketing, it means clear messages and clean proposals to consumers and industry customers.

In public relations, it means clear, forthright messages.

CHAPTER 5:

The Best Ways to Work with the Media

You are going to want to expand your roster of media contacts and, at the same time, *keep* every one you get. Gaining media contacts is most easily accomplished by helping those busy reporters and producers do their jobs. The fastest way to help someone working in the media is by not wasting their precious time. Creating fruitful, productive and warm relationships with reporters and producers is a two-way street. If you make their jobs easier, and respect their time and the constraints on it—including deadlines—you'll also be helping yourself. Start with being well-prepared before you attempt to engage a reporter, use your resources wisely, and know how to recognize and take advantage of opportunities that your competitors don't see or utilize. This chapter will give you smart ideas for winning relationships with media professionals.

SMART IDEA: Practice your pitch before you make the pitch.

When you set out to engage with anyone in the media, make sure beforehand that you have a well-written, well-rehearsed and short pitch requiring no more than 45 seconds to speak or read. Getting your pitch down to three or four sentences is essential if you seek to capture anyone's attention. Think about movie or book summaries: they sum up the plot in a few sentences to make you want to see that movie or read that book. In the same way, you need a grabber, a sound bite that will make the fish take the bait. Mark Twain famously said, "If I had more time I would have written you a shorter letter." With pitches, make plenty of notes and brainstorm with others until you unearth your most engaging catchphrases. The goal is to make your opening gambit memorable when you speak with a media person—or more likely, when you leave the first voicemail. You want that call back! Likewise, whatever you come up with should also be part of a well-written paragraph or two that you start using for email pitches.

Once you have your copy down and are happy with it, practice saying it aloud with someone you trust. Every call you make to a media person is important, so don't just wing it. You should have a summary paragraph in front of you and a list of bullet points of what you want to convey. After all, you might be lucky enough to reach the person you're calling on the first try and have an immediate opportunity to expand your pitch into a full discussion of why you are media coverage-worthy.

This said, don't read or simply memorize a prepared pitch. Rehearse it like a great actor. The idea is to know your story by heart and speak naturally with heartfelt passion. People can tell the difference between someone who is enthusiastic about their company assets and someone who is merely reciting. If you sound conversational, a listener is more likely to want to hear more and enter into a discussion. A "canned" exchange that feels artificial will be a big turnoff, especially to time-starved media types.

There's no need to be pushy with your pitch. If someone says no, go to the next person on your target list. If the person you called suggests you call back, say you will and ask when the best time might be. And *do* call back.

However, a bit more advice on this topic: don't worry if a machine picks up. Don't hang up. Remember—phone calls are very powerful. You can deliver your message right into that person's ear via their receiver. There are few times in life you will ever get this close to strangers. But do not keep leaving voicemails with the exact same message. Be sure to vary it creatively and keep your enthusiasm extra-high.

SMART IDEA: Respect the deadlines and time constraints of the media.

The secret to winning amazing placements and large volumes of media coverage is this: understand and respect the challenges reporters face. Genuinely respecting their job often makes the difference between getting a story featured in a coveted outlet or not.

You show respect by realizing that reporters like to see their names at the top of a leading story. They want recognition too. Yet while they are striving to make a name as an established reporter, producer or writer in a highly competitive arena, it is quite likely they are being underpaid for their talent and contributions. Add that overwork and constant deadlines come with their territory, and you begin to understand their daily grind.

View it as your job to help the media do their jobs, and your likelihood of garnering more and greater story placements will rise. More so, doing this is the best way to show respect for the reporter, their time and challenges.

Reporters need story ideas. At the same time, most of them get pitched all day long via phone, email, snail mail, FedEx, fax and blog comment, by others who likewise want to see their news in print. This being the case, how do you increase your odds? Make your story as compelling as possible from the audience's perspective!

I noted that a respectful relationship with a reporter begins when you hone your pitch to no more than 45 seconds *before* you pick up the phone to sell your story angle. Next, you must describe exactly why your story is worthwhile from their audience's perspective. Remember—the reporter has to deliver stories that their outlet's readers or viewers want. If you miss this essential point, you aren't being very respectful and you are wasting that reporter's time.

Once you spark a reporter's interest, you might be asked for additional information that you don't have at your fingertips. That's okay. Don't feel compelled to make anything up or guess. Delivering the right facts for a story to get properly developed is essential. The point is that once you have a reporter intrigued or "hooked" on doing a story, it becomes your responsibility to get back to them with the information they request within the timeframe discussed—not later. Never make a reporter pick up the phone to remind you that they need certain facts to complete their story. This alone is a surefire way to get your story dropped—or have its tone distinctly change!

If you do not intend to provide certain information, say so up front. Repeat your position if necessary. They'll understand. Good reporters are inquisitive. They'll try their darndest to get the story angle they seek. This doesn't mean you have to cave or say anything you aren't prepared to announce or substantiate. Don't pretend you'll provide a reporter with information you have no intention of delivering. This will only destroy your credibility and might create unnecessary curiosity about why you want to hold back the requested information.

Practice the basics of Respect 101. You'll be rewarded with more and better media coverage.

SMART IDEA: Increase the reach of your story and do it frequently.

In the context of media, *reach* means the actual number of people or percentage of your target audience that will actually read about or hear your story. *Frequency* relates to how many times these people will be exposed to it.

You need both.

Reach and frequency are the reasons why an effective media campaign is not limited solely to a few major national media outlets, but instead must also target trade, local radio stations and local newspapers across the country while you wait for your big break in a national print or broadcast outlet.

Let's delve into this. Major national media often have news bureaus in several cities. I'd recommend submitting all your news stories to major newspapers and magazines twice: one copy to the main editorial office, the other to the nearest local bureau. This doubles the chances that the media will respond to your news release. It is the local bureau's job to find newsworthy local events, people and products. If the local thinks your story is worth covering, national headquarters might pick it up too. Of course, if the news is significant enough, it can also work in reverse—national first, local second.

Studies show that most people need to see your message seven times or more before it begins to sink in and can be recognized and recalled. Advertising legend David Ogilvy named this "The Law of Seven."

Never discredit those "little placements." There are consumers in little towns across the world, reading their local newspapers. In the aggregate, lots of little stories will ultimately help take your overall message to an ever-widening audience, especially if, as a direct or indirect result, you do get the big national placement. Also, as we'll delve into later, all those little placements can do wonders for your "search-ability" via Internet search engines.

SMART IDEA: Selectively distribute your media kits.

In newsrooms around the world, unsolicited media kits are typically tossed in the garbage.

So should you prepare and distribute an expensive press kit that is highly likely to be thrown out?

Media kits are useful tools, but they should be selectively distributed to those who have actually requested them. More so, they should be offered in both print and electronic format prior to sending. Let your media contacts know they are available; ask if they would like them emailed or snail mailed—but don't foist them on anybody prior to the request for more information.

A well-written, well-designed highlights sheet that clearly and suc-cinctly details what you are promoting, coupled with crisp product images if applicable, might help you achieve greater media coverage. More extensive brochures can always be sent after your highlights sheet or pitch letter intrigues someone and they're asking for more.

A highlights sheet is ideally limited to one or two pages in an easy-to-read format with a legible standard font. Black letters on white paper work just fine. Remember—you might be emailing these, so the less toner cartridge required for printing, the better.

A point worth noting: if you are preparing a one-pager for your publicly traded company, avoid the common temptation of calling your flyer a "fact sheet." Accept that it is likely a highlights sheet and name it accordingly. I can't imagine you'll be inclined to include "facts" that might be low points. By neglecting to point out certain facts on a doc-ument called a "fact sheet," you might be accused of failing to impart information that could be deemed material to an investment decision.

SMART IDEA: Use "slow" weeks of the year to your advantage.

Lots of people take vacations the last week of August and the week between Christmas and New Year's Day. Consequently, a common assumption is that it is a waste of time to reach out to the media during these weeks. This rationale is flawed. Holidays and common vacation weeks can present unique opportunities for great media coverage, if you choose to act while your competitors might be resting.

Typically, whether print or online, newspapers publish 365 days a year. They need suitable news and editorial content to frame the advertisements that constitute the mainstay of their revenues. Likewise, television, cable, radio and web-based news sites need to run their regular programming whether or not there is a holiday or vacation week. The news outlets of the world do not stop and go on vacation, nor can they afford to tell their advertisers they won't be publishing that day or week—or those advertisers would take their money elsewhere.

Unless required to disseminate news due to material corporate developments, some companies refrain from reaching out to reporters or issuing press releases during holidays because they feel their news might not reach a broad audience. You might agree, but you will likely miss some great opportunities. Just imagine those lonely reporters who are working the holiday shift, sitting at their desks receiving far fewer calls than usual, fewer emails and fewer news releases. They're waiting for some news!

The public seeks news every day of the year. Get your media pitches out during the holidays when your less media-savvy competition might be vacationing. Here are some ways you can take advantage of slow weeks:

1. Refine the messages that make you an expert in your field. Write at least one media alert highlighting your spokesperson's area of expertise and distribute it. During holidays, the usual "go-to experts" might be vacationing, which presents the ideal opportunity for qualified people to "audition"—via an actual news segment—as a new and reliable commentator on an event or industry.

2. Write at least one feature release about some aspect of your business that you believe would appeal to the masses. Make the story "evergreen" so the outlet can run it as space allows.

3. Update your media kit and/or website. If the changes are sufficiently dramatic, put out a release highlighting the updates.

4. Prepare a commentary piece on news developments concerning your   industry in general. Disseminate it.

5. Budget for a public relations campaign. The end of the year is an ideal time to put aside some money for image-building for the year ahead. At my company, we readily turn an annual $100,000+ public relations investment into millions of dollars in advertising equivalency for our clients. The resulting publicity value is priceless.

SMART IDEA: Publicity generates more publicity.

Few companies' public relations teams realize they can and should capitalize on media attention by putting out a press release announcing they are in the news!

Yes, you read that right. If your company is featured in a prestigious newspaper or magazine article, why not put out a press release letting your usual followers—and the rest of the world—know you are featured in that story? While you're at it, make sure you credit the reporter by name, and tag them in your social media announcements as well—much more about this in Part II. This underutilized tactic works and is an easy way to increase your media presence and enhance your reputation—especially with investors.

Publicity begets more publicity. Once you get the ball rolling, it will often continue rolling by itself.

SMART IDEA: Beware of gifting the media.

It feels great to give a present. However, don't succumb to the temptation to send gifts to reporters, producers or others in a position to write or publish a story about you, your company or your most recent news. Most print and broadcast outlets have strict ethical standard policies, which include not accepting gifts.

If you want to express thanks *after* a placement, consider sending a carefully worded thank-you note to the newsroom. This is always in good taste, and does not compromise policy. Few people use this time-honored, classy tradition, but it will help you be remembered. Other acceptable gifts might include something home-baked and hand-delivered or promotional items with your company's name and logo on them—items you would use for ordinary marketing and branding purposes.

Another great way to say thanks is to utilize social media. Mention the reporter's name and the article in your tweets with a tag (@) before the reporter's name or Twitter handle—more on this in Part II. This online recognition is always appreciated and welcomed.

Keep the basics of this rule in mind when meeting a reporter for a meal as well. Don't pick the most expensive place. Be moderate in your selection. Often, the publisher or news station's policy is to pick up the check. Just as you would not want to be remembered as a big shot who appeared to bribe someone with good food and drink, neither do you want to be remembered as an inconsiderate person who did not respect a limited expense account. As in most things, good judgment is prudent.

SMART IDEA: Install a toll-free number.

If you are serious about providing customer service and support, and attracting media attention, that determination should come through clearly in your public relations and marketing campaigns. One easy way to do this is to install a toll-free number. Toll-free numbers make it easier for your customers to call and order from you. Also, many reporters are freelancing and working stories at their own expense, so toll-free calls are appreciated. Such numbers are inexpensive nowadays, and you really can't afford to offer anything less.

If you do install a toll-free number, be sure to include it in all your outreach. Make it available to customers and contacts. Have it printed on your sales literature, catalogs, news releases and other outgoing mail. If you are selling something, be sure to include it on your order forms.

The advantages of toll-free numbers are that they:

1. Make it more convenient for customers to order from you
2. Speed ordering response
3. Have been documented to triple offer responses
4. Produce larger orders
5. Encourage impulse calls
6. Build goodwill

Lastly, a toll-free number might allow you to better track your public relations campaign results.

Always make sure someone reliable and articulate is answering your phones. The inbound caller is forming a permanent perception of your company. When reporters return your calls, if they can't get a person on the phone but instead get mired in an automated voicemail maze, they might give up—and hang up. Personally, nothing drives me crazier than automated voicemail. My office does not have voicemail during office hours. While we're there, I insist that a live person, not a recording, must handle every call.

CHAPTER 6:

Power & Punch
That Makes the
Cover(age) Difference

A well-written press release can be the catalyst that starts a productive dialogue with a reporter or producer you have been unable to reach by telephone. There are a variety of elements to consider as you sit down to write copy that will trigger immediate coverage or inspire an interview request, resulting in a more in-depth article. In this chapter, we will explore how a professionally written announcement can win the reader's attention.

SMART IDEA: Keep your message simple.

The 24/7/365 bombardment of images, sounds and texts we all experience can be invigorating, exhausting or both. Today, many of the listeners you seek are retreating from this onslaught to maintain focus and sanity.

To communicate effectively today, you must cut through the clutter or "noise level" by capturing attention in the clearest, simplest, most memorable ways. This will help to create a positive impact on your targeted listener or viewer. If a fifth grader would struggle to understand the significance of your press release, change it. Simplify, simplify, simplify.

SMART IDEA: You've got about five seconds to catch a reporter's attention.

Polls show that editors, reporters and producers spend an average of five seconds reading a news release before deciding whether to use it or trash it.

With every announcement you make, decide how you are going to get the essence of your news into the first sentence of your first paragraph while making that all-important "sound bite" exciting.

Those long, wordy press releases you've been writing are largely a waste of time, paper and money. Want greater coverage? Never forget this five-second rule of engagement.

SMART IDEA: Put your "hook" in the headline.

The lyrics of the song "The Hook" by Blues Traveler declared: "The hook brings you back, on that you can rely." Although the songwriter might have been referencing "Peter Pan" or musing on personal interpretations of song lyrics, the line holds true for press releases, songs, stories, jokes and anything else you offer with hopes of capturing attention. If you neglect to put your hook in the headline, you will miss great opportunities for media coverage.

Time is precious. Readers don't want to waste their time any more than you want others to waste yours. If the story's hook isn't readily apparent, if the compelling reason to keep reading isn't right at the top of the page, the reader will likely move on to another, more interesting story that better respects their time.

Seek creative ways to present yourself, your company and your news. Although the format for press releases might be fairly standard, you can still make your news stand out with a well-expressed angle—the "hook"—along with fresh framing and descriptive words. Look for a new hook every time you write a release. Albert Einstein's definition of insanity was doing the same thing over and over again while expecting different results. Don't fall into that trap. Freshen up!

SMART IDEA: One-page press releases are the best.

I said this before, but it bears repeating: the length of your press release is very important. Anything longer than one page—unless it is a release that requires financial tables—is giving the reader permission to ignore you. Overly long releases usually inspire reactions counter to those you desire. First, they'll inspire the reader to move on to something more interesting, such as someone else's news release! Second, they are more likely to create confusion, which will flatline the heartbeat of your story.

The most successful news release is tightly written and about 300 to 500 words long. Religiously use "Word Count" in whatever writing application you use. If media are seeking something more extensive, they will specifically ask you for it: it's called an interview!

SMART IDEA: Capture attention or lose the opportunity to do so.

If you live in New York City or any place that sells the *New York Post*, you are familiar with the creative ability of its headline writers to catch eyes and demand attention. The headlines inspire a read, chuckle or groan—and lots of subsequent chatter. To master the *Post's* style, think: **C**oncise, **S**urprising, **T**rue and **P**rovocative. If you can hit all four, you've nailed it!

What kind of titles work? Take a look at these legendary Post headlines:

Tiger Admits: I'm a Cheetah
Woods' wife attacked him with wedge!
(Headline about Tiger Woods' affair)

H-OLÉ!...and Yet He Lived to Tell About It!
(Headline about a bullfighter who was impaled)

TEXAS HOLD UP
25G poker debt sparked duel
(Gilbert Arenas busted for pulling guns on teammate in locker room due to gambling debt)

LADY IS A TRUMP
3rd wife's the charm
(Headline announcing The Donald's marriage to model Melania)

World Cup Shocker
USA WINS 1-1
Best tie against the British since Bunker Hill
(This could be the most accurate and inaccurate headline ever. How can you win a tie game? Claiming to win a tie is genius. Comparing it to Bunker Hill? Priceless!)

OSAMA BIN WANKIN'!
It's Whora Bora—porn found in Laden's foxhole
(A groan-inducing but heavily talked-about headline that needs no explanation)

How can you capture attention by being concise, surprising, true and provocative in your next headline?

SMART IDEA: Stop the jargon. Use plain English.

Why write "a means of egress" and then have to define "egress," when you can write "a way to get out" or "exit" in the first place?

There is power in simple, straightforward language. Simplifying something technical means you really have to understand it. Writers who don't understand what they are writing about often regurgitate technical terms to try and mask their lack of understanding. This does a disservice to your company and your readers—the audiences you seek to serve.

Avoid complicated language, unless you are writing a technical piece for a technically sophisticated audience. Jargon won't impress a lay audience.

Never put a word you wouldn't normally use into a press release or any other written material. It might confuse many and doesn't advance your cause.

SMART IDEA: Choose your adjectives, adverbs and punctuation carefully.

Well-placed adjectives and adverbs are necessary for style and effect.

For example, as it was once pointed out to me, Article II, Section I of the United States Constitution would certainly read differently without its adverbs: "I do *solemnly* swear (or affirm) that I will *faithfully* execute the Office of President of the United States…"

However, watch out for overkill. Keep your sentences simple and elegant with a few adjectives and adverbs that help the reader understand the value of whatever news you are sharing.

Hone your use of commas. For example, "Eat, Grandma" without the comma is advocating cannibalism.

Also, punctuate for clarity and watch the use of exclamation points. Let the reader decide the impact and significance of your words.

Ignore this idea and you risk being perceived as too promotional and lacking sincerity.

SMART IDEA: Use quotes for subjective comments and emphasis.

All facts belong in the body of the press release, with the most important facts in paragraph #1...but you already know that.

Subjective comments—which you offer as speculation or opinion—belong in quotes.

It's a common error in news releases to put the actual news in the quote of the CEO or President. This is a BIG mistake!

Facts, the news, must always stand alone. Quotations are the editorial notes of a press release, where the writer can elaborate on why the news is important and relevant to the company, the industry, investors, consumers, partners or the world-at-large. Between quotation marks is where publicly traded companies can take more liberties with highlighting aspects of the news that would benefit from emphasis.

In addition to highlighting your own perspectives in quotes, further quotes from other industry experts can help strengthen your news announcements. These added commentaries will also make a release read more like a regular news story.

Quotes allow you to strengthen points that might require elaboration or context.

Before you hit the send button and share your news with the world, reread your release carefully. Make sure the main facts are in the headline and first paragraph and the quotations merely provide more color to help readers grasp the impact of your news.

SMART IDEA: Lose the fluff.

This is so important I might have to say it a few more times: do radical surgery on your copy if you must. Reporters have a limited amount of time, face constant deadlines and know poop when they see it.

The reporter who reads much beyond the headline and first paragraph of a news release is rare.

So lose the fluff in your releases. Instead, give your release a strong lead that grabs the reader's attention. A news release should read like a standard news story. It must answer the questions: What? Who? Why? Where? When? How? These questions should be answered in an inverted pyramid style—with the most important facts first, moving down to the least important. Pithy quotations from company spokespersons will carry much more credibility if they say something about the actual news or event, rather than telling readers that you are "excited, delighted or thrilled." You'd better be excited, delighted or thrilled—otherwise, why are you making the announcement? Use quotes to put the news into the context of your big vision for the future.

SMART IDEA: Proofread and proofread again.

Grammatical and spelling errors are significant barriers to getting your news published. Computer spell-checks have their uses, but always check your spelling the good old-fashioned ways as well—with a second set of eyes and a dictionary. There are several dictionaries online. I especially like www.m-w.com and www.dictionary.com.

Your computer's spell-check function won't catch the error when you call your CEO "bald" instead of "bold," but readers will surely notice. They will have a laugh at your expense and then question your professionalism, since only amateurs rely exclusively on spell-check. Keep your proofreading skills sharp, and proofread your press releases multiple times, using several sets of eyes, before you release anything to the public. Check not only for misspelled words, but also for errors in sentence structure.

Consider these blunders, adapted from *500 Clean Jokes and Humorous Stories and How to Tell Them* by Rusty Wright and Linda Raney Wright (Barbour Publishing, 1998), and make sure you don't make any in your news releases or other materials:

- ❖ Newspaper headline: "Two convicts evade noose, jury hung."
- ❖ Sign in laundromat: "We don't tear your laundry in our machines. We do it by hand."
- ❖ Hospital notices: "William Anderson was released yesterday from the hospital where his right leg was placed in a cast following a fracture of his left ankle."
- ❖ "Arthur Edwards left Park Street Hospital Wednesday, still recovering from a head injury and shock caused by coming into contact with a live wife."

SMART IDEA: Be willing to write a matte story.

A matte story is a release you write that is placed on news syndication wires. Matte stories are usually 400 to 600 words long and tied into a trend or angle that will resonate with a wide audience. They are written just like news articles, but include your company name and one or more quotes from you or your spokesperson as the main expert for the story.

A matte story is a particular kind of news release that is guaranteed a certain amount of media coverage. The cost per release can range from $200 to more than $5,500. Syndicators offer these articles to newspapers, websites and reporters, while granting permission to reprint the story verbatim. Some syndicators offer editors, producers and reporters royalty-free online downloading of your submitted story so it can reside on their websites. Others use push methods to deliver your content to subscribing reporters and producers.

Matte stories can be extremely effective when initiating a national awareness campaign. The articles are copyright-free and in the public domain. No permission is necessary to reprint them. They sometimes appear in newspapers and look like any other newspaper article. They might also look like a column and have a border around them. This type of matte release usually has a headline that says "Breaking Health News," "News for Women," "New Advances in Technology" or something equally general and enticing. These roundup stories are customarily picked up by smaller dailies or suburban papers hungry for content and lacking the larger reporting staffs more common to large regionals or national papers.

Do not underestimate the impact of these lower-circulation papers. These could be "the only news in town." They offer the potential of having your story read by hundreds of thousands or even millions of people. Also, if the stories are appealing enough and written as "evergreens," they sometimes remain in circulation for years.

Editors love matte releases if you've provided sound, interesting, useful, well-presented, educational, entertaining information without a blatant pitch. You are helping the outlet's production budget by doing their work for them! The outlets are helping you with third-party endorsement coverage within the pages of their papers. Don't be surprised if a great many publications run your story and your phones start ringing.

SMART IDEA: Follow the standard release format for corporate news.

Here is the basic outline for a standard media news release. To use a legal turn of phrase, ignore this format at your own risk:

FOR IMMEDIATE RELEASE

Or FOR RELEASE AT WILL

Or FOR RELEASE: [date]

(Use a release date if it shouldn't be run before a specific date.)

Contact:

First Name, Last Name

Title
Company Name
Phone Number
Email address (Optional: see * below)
Headline
Subheadline

Tell the entire story in the headline and subhead. Get straight to the point. Give your headline punch and have your subhead fill in the details.

CITY, STATE (Date) – The lead paragraph contains the news and is ideally one sentence long (the who, what, when, where and why information). Craft a solid, hard-hitting opening that is written in third-person, pure journalistic style while being completely free of hyperbole.

A few supporting paragraphs follow, including a relevant quote or two from key management.

Concluding paragraph, which, if possible, is a call to action.

Also include an "About..." This is boilerplate about your company, including your website address.

Include Safe Harbor language, if necessary. That's legalese for a provision to reduce or eliminate liability as long as good faith is demonstrated. This usually has to do with financial projections and ability to fulfill business objectives. When in doubt, consult your attorney. For Safe Harbor language to hold up in court, it must reflect the news in the press release.

When writing news releases, keep in mind these three basic components:

1. The headline must be a compelling and concise statement that encapsulates the main ideas of the release. A good subhead often offers concrete information.
2. The first paragraph repeats and expands on the headline's theme.
3. What follows is supporting documentation, such as approved

quotes from management, a customer or another party—especially those available for possible interviews.

If you are seriously thinking about undertaking the public relations efforts yourself, get a copy of the official Associated Press (AP) Stylebook—and be sure to follow the AP style rules if you want quality coverage.

*Email Address: Including your email address is optional. If the release is being disseminated exclusively to the media, absolutely include one. However, if the release will go out to investors or the public-at-large, you might prefer to not include an email address. You can get deluged by spammers and emails that you cannot answer due to Regulation Fair Disclosure (Reg FD), which prohibits selective disclosure. Instead of annoying people by having to tell them you "can't" answer their emailed questions—which will be perceived as you "won't"—why not avoid the issue altogether by simply not offering an email address in these cases?

SMART IDEA: Know the outlet *before* pitching.

Many so-called public relations folks make very serious and potentially highly damaging mistakes when pitching their company or other clients.

They pitch using blast emails or mass mailing—without carefully considering the recipient. My company has been hired many times to resolve the crisis that inevitably results after a willy-nilly amateur firm blasted out news indiscriminately—only to have a contrarian reporter receive the news release and proceed to publish an incendiary opposing opinion piece with more than a little damaging impact.

Blast emails are gone like the dinosaurs. We'll go into this in detail in Part II. For mailed or emailed pitches that are sent with the goal of obtaining press coverage, you *must* research the publication, understand its focus and know the reporter's interest before sending an email. Make sure the subject line fits that reporter's personal "beat" or focus. Then send your email.

SMART IDEA: Include a photo with your releases. Make it a face when possible.

Years ago, in a letter to readers, the publisher of a national magazine noted: "As is often the case, eye-catching photography was crucial to our choice of subject coverage. The strength of a picture will often make or break a story item…we want unusual subjects doing unusual things." Visuals help.

Press releases with a good photo tend to get better pickup than those without images. People like to "see" what they are reading about. They like to read about how products or companies are impacting people. Photos put a "face" on your story. A news release that highlights a person in an interesting way increases your chances of media pickup.

At my company, we use photos whenever possible with every release. Sometimes the photos are of our client's products, facilities or management team. At other times, we might source and license an inexpensive photo that helps tell the story better. Check out www.fotolia.com and open an account. There you can scroll through an immense, well-organized database of photographs, sketches and images for just about any topic and purchase credits to buy them.

SMART IDEA: Make sure that your information is 100 percent accurate.

Fudged facts will come back to haunt you. When you put anything in writing, checking and double-checking your factual statements is a must. Anything less will most likely get you into trouble.

Cite your references. If you've presented fiction as fact in *any* form, a reporter aspiring to greater success will eventually find out. Don't ever assume that reporters won't do plenty of legwork to authenticate your claims. Credible and/or hungry reporters will authenticate. Then the outlet's editors will do it again!

SMART IDEA: If you must translate your releases into other languages, make sure you use someone who is a superior linguist. Always be sure to check and double-check the translation for possible alternative meanings.

Do not rely on Google or any other automated software for accurate translation of your press releases. Hire a professional if translating is necessary. Translating your news into multiple languages is a task that can challenge even highly skilled language pros.

A few classic errors that highlight the need for using a native translator include:

- ❖ The Pepsi slogan "Come Alive with the Pepsi Generation," when marketed in Taiwan, was translated as "Pepsi will bring your ancestors back from the dead."
- ❖ When the Pope visited Miami, one t-shirt seller printed shirts in Spanish saying "I saw the potato."
- ❖ Chevy's Nova sold wonderfully in the U.S. market while bombing in Spanish-speaking markets since "no va" translates to "doesn't go."
- ❖ In Arabic, the Jolly Green Giant translates to "Intimidating Green Ogre."
- ❖ Clairol's Mist Stick for women's hairstyling, when translated into German, ran into a problem since "mist" means "manure" in German.

In translation, it gets down to this: the nuance of the word might be more important than the verbatim translation.

CHAPTER 7:

How Smart Public Companies Become Intelligently Transparent

Whenever you work for, or on behalf of, any publicly traded company, you're going to have to put out news about the company's finances. This can sometimes feel like you are walking a tightrope across a yawning chasm in a high wind. The tension leading up to the event is understandable, but accurate financial news reporting is a necessary part of your job. I'd like to help you see it in perspective, while I cannot overemphasize the importance of full attention toward this make-or-break process. The media and investors want financial information, and you have to give it to them in the most accurate way you can. If, as you read on, you don't understand any of the terms* in the ideas in this chapter, it is your duty to educate yourself. These are rules you need to follow not just well but *perfectly* in order to write releases about your company's finances. (*In my companion book *FUNDaMentals: The Corporate Guide to Cultivating Investor Mindshare*, there is an extensive glossary of financial terms.)

SMART IDEA: Focus your messaging on controllable factors in your company.

More than 10 years later, an article that appeared in the July 1, 2003 issue of the *Harvard Business Review* still resonates. In "Delusions of Success: How Optimism Underscores Executive Decisions," authors Dan Lovallo and Daniel Kahneman suggest we "tend to exaggerate the degree of control we have over events, discounting the role of luck." The article documents this phenomenon using investor relations and provides a rational explanation.

"A study of letters to shareholders in annual reports," the authors write, "found that executives tend to attribute favorable outcomes to factors under their control, such as their corporate strategy or their R&D programs. Unfavorable outcomes, by contrast, were more likely to be attributable to uncontrollable external factors such as weather or inflation."

Such overoptimism can be a virtue in corporate leaders reporting to their shareholders and the public, but this attitude can also inadvertently lead to misunderstandings.

To avoid marketplace confusion, which will typically flatline or tank a stock chart, focus on controllable factors in your messaging. For example, if you want to acknowledge that certain external factors have impacted your quarter, immediately assess your strategy for addressing or reducing their impact going forward.

Outside of very specific times, blaming inflation, the weather or any other uncontrollable force is a waste of energy and does nothing for your credibility. The message is better told by specifically addressing what actions you have taken and/or will be taking to improve performance now and in the future, in light of the current environment. If you can't figure out how to do this and relay your choices concisely, don't expect your investor base to feel comfortable remaining on the deck of what might be a sinking ship.

SMART IDEA: Break out from the pack by making your "Management's Discussion and Analysis of Financial Condition and Results of Operations"—the MD&A section of your 10-K filing—truly informative.

All information that investors need in order to evaluate your company's results must be included in the "Management's Discussion and Analysis" (MD&A) section of 10-K and 10-Q filings. This information is often discussed in conference calls and in U.S. Securities and Exchange Commission (SEC) filings, but omitted from press releases. These omissions only make it harder for investors to obtain the information they desire—and might inspire them to transform into Sherlock Holmes or simply lose interest.

The SEC, in its interpretive guidelines, proposes that the key purposes of the MD&A are to:

1. Provide a narrative explanation of a company's financial statements, enabling investors to see the company through the eyes of management

2. Enhance overall financial disclosure and provide context for analysis

3. Provide information about the quality and variability of a company's earnings and cash flow

For you to be one of the relatively few companies that shares its annual MD&A in a more exciting and candid way would be wildly refreshing to the media—but even more significantly, to your present and potential investors. Certainly consult with your legal advisor, but try to keep this news release exciting. Start by sharing a series of highlights that help you shine in the eyes of your current and potential shareholders. Move on to the challenges you've faced and wrap up with your vision for the future before attaching your accurate and carefully formatted financial tables.

SMART IDEA: Improve your transparency to build media and shareholder trust.

Want to build your credibility with the media? Follow these earnings reporting guidelines.

At a minimum, earnings announcements should include both a complete Income Statement and a complete Balance Sheet. The Income Statement should include data for the current quarter, comparison to the prior-year quarter and, if informative—as in reflecting a trend—to a sequentially previous quarter with similar comparisons for the year-to-date. The Balance Sheet should include data for the current period and the prior fiscal year-end and, again, if informative, comparisons with the prior-year comparable period. This disclosure gives investors the information needed to determine free cash flow and the company's ability to meet its financial requirements. Put generally accepted accounting principles (GAAP) earnings up front in any release. In fact, GAAP earnings should appear in the first paragraph. *Only* GAAP earnings should appear in headlines of a release.

Also, be sure to keep these key points in mind:

❖ Always include a brief description of the company's business that clarifies how you make money.

❖ Outline trends that are causing or might cause revenues to increase, decrease or remain flat.

❖ Include a brief discussion of what dynamics drive other significant business factors.

❖ Explain charges—both pre-tax and after-tax numbers—and state whether there will be or could be similar charges again in the future.

❖ Discuss liquidity and capital resources. Include debt levels and key ratios, adequacy of cash resources, cash from operations, capital expenditures, any anticipated changes in charges in financing and share repurchase plans, if any.

❖ Offer measurements that allow the reader to assess your ongoing success.

❖ Disclose any material changes in accounting practices you adopted during the quarter, either due to changes in Financial Accounting Standards Board (FASB) requirements or by company choice.

❖ State the company's current expectations for sales and earnings as clearly and honestly as possible.

The idea is to help people learn more about your company. To this end, provide your financial statements as Excel files. This will make it easier for readers to get an unambiguous picture of your financials. Do this even if you don't have anything but losses at the time.

Ultimately, you cannot fool everyone about losses—nor should you ever try. There is no long-term benefit to be gained from avoiding the facts. Help investors see the financial story for what it currently is and where you think it is going, along with your plans for executing on that vision. Just making your financial statements available in accessible file format will set you apart from your competitors—because so few have the guts to do it.

Believe it or not, even not-so-great quarters are an opportunity to build your credibility.

SMART IDEA: Write financial releases as if you work for *People* magazine.

Stop listening to your lawyers. (Did I really say that?) I'm not telling you to *ignore* your lawyers' advice. Heaven forbid! What I'm saying is, cut the boring legalese unless it has been determined that using it is your only option. Instead, get to the point in your financial releases in the most comprehensible, easy-to-read way that you can.

Unfortunately, too many releases about quarterly finance updates read as if an attorney wrote them—possibly because they *did*. When you lift sentences or paragraphs verbatim from a lawyer's composition, you're not going to wind up with a release that is easy to grasp. Plus, it might be so dull it challenges attention spans before you have the opportunity to impart other developments!

When writing a quarterly financial release, make sure that you—or whoever is writing it—truly understands the information well enough to communicate the news simply and directly.

One effective way to get to the point in a financial release is by opening with a few bullet points highlighting advances the company has made during the quarter or year. Then begin your financial discussion in a way that will be comprehensible to the average reader. I call this a *People* magazine or *USA Today* writing style.

If your attorneys insist on complicating matters, let their jargon appear in latter paragraphs of the press release—since most people only read the first two or three paragraphs of a release closely and skim the rest.

Simple steps like these will allow you to stand out in the crowded field of 12,000 publicly traded companies—of which seven out of 10 have market capitalizations under $500 million. Create distinction with superior reporting.

CHAPTER 8:

Show & Tell

Some CEOs view media interviews and corporate presentations as an interruption of their workday or a waste of time. In reality, these activities are essential and relied upon by many to assess company leadership—which might be why some officers don't care for them. If you can't deliver energetic and commanding speeches or polished and articulate interviews, you are short-circuiting your company's future. There is no time like the present to do something to improve the situation.

This chapter will help you gear up so you can take better advantage of the opportunities that require public speaking.

SMART IDEA: Craft a short, simple corporate presentation.

Lincoln's Gettysburg Address helped change the nation and the world. It was less than 300 words. If a modern newscaster were to deliver that speech at their average pace of 150 to 170 words a minute, the speech would be over in two minutes.

Keep your presentation simple, keep it short and add value with relevant slides either via PowerPoint, Pages or the format of your choice. Use images to impart your message vs. word-copy whenever possible. If you'd like it to be valuable enough to be used as the basis for hand-outs you leave with your audience, add enough detail so each page is relevant. Otherwise, consider preparing an Executive Summary as a brochure instead which is often more valuable.

Take it from me (and this is long experience talking, the result of having gone on many road shows with CEOs): No matter how amazing you are as a presenter, you need to be able to grasp attention in 5 minutes or less and keep that attention while you tell your company's story in 15 minutes or less. This is usually all the time even the best speakers have before the audience starts to tune out. After 15 or 20 minutes, unless the presentation has become very interactive, you are commanding only a tiny amount of your audience's attention span.

Don't waste anyone's precious time by droning on as you recite information listed on PowerPoint slides. Remember, you control whether your presentation is a waste of time or not. Keep your verbal and visual content interesting. You're on stage and your role is to paraphrase the key messages while adding color, dimension and context.

It is a good practice to make sure your most recent corporate presentation is posted on your website for easy access. For the record, always ask before emailing a file as large as the typical PowerPoint presentation. Many people are reluctant to open an attachment unless they know exactly whom it is from and why it was sent. You surely don't want your email address to be moved to a permanent spam file. Alternatively, a good practice would be to send out an email to potentially interested recipients and let them know exactly where they can view the presentation on your website. Hopefully you'll have plenty of other compelling information for them to read once you get their undivided attention.

SMART IDEA: Follow this four-step rule for all public speaking engagements.

Increase your success during public speaking engagements by following these four steps for improving your audience's receptivity:

1. Share a brief personal or relevant story.
2. Explain the connection of that story to what you intend to say.
3. Present your succinctly crafted message.
4. Recap your talk by telling them what makes you or your company compelling.

You can evaluate the effectiveness of your speech before you give it by recording it. There are plenty of inexpensive recording apps you can easily download to rehearse and perfect your speech. If it seems wordy or overlong, keep honing the message until you get it down to a few essential paragraphs, thoughts, bullet points or sound bites. Ask others you trust to listen to a few run-throughs. These exercises will determine whether your speech gets to the point, while helping you deliver your message in an interesting and memorable manner.

Investors and the media have very little patience. Time is money for all of us. So perform.

SMART IDEA: Practice makes perfect. Rehearse. Then rehearse again.

Well-rehearsed speakers tend to deliver presentations far superior to those delivered by speakers who "wing it."

Numerous selective disclosure rules prohibit you, as management, from revealing any new material information at selective one-on-one meetings.

If and when you decide to break your news to the world-at-large—especially if you decide to relay it via news conference—you will want to make sure you have carefully thought about the wording, and also rehearsed its delivery.

Rehearsing helps you become more comfortable with both tone and questions because, with practice, you will have ready answers. The more you rehearse, the more relaxed you will be when confronted with a question you might not want to answer—since you have an answer prepared anyway.

Investors are looking for honest, credible management teams that effectively impart not only their vision, but also their ability to deliver on that vision.

Great speakers are like people who are great at anything—they practice constantly. Watch any professional athlete. Although some people might have more innate skill than others, those who want to stay on top know full well that practice makes perfect. Or as All-Star National Hockey League player Alex Ovechkin says, "Practice doesn't make perfect. Perfect practice makes perfect."

SMART IDEA: Television flattens voices, so make sure yours is energized.

Whether you are booked on a television or radio show, or are webcasting a conference call, make sure you bring 100 percent enthusiasm to the forum. If you don't, nobody will stick around to listen or watch you long enough to hear your message.

Enthusiasm is contagious—people feel it, hear it, see it and want it. If you express yourself enthusiastically, it will draw others to you and compel them to listen with equal energy. The expression in your voice will sell your ideas more effectively than any other aspect of the sales process. When you speak with power and passion, you naturally convey excitement, which, in turn, excites other people into response. I believe the passion and excitement I have for my profession—perfecting the public communications process—has resulted in more business for my companies over the years than even our glowing references. And when potential clients encounter the enthusiastic professionals I surround myself with at my current company, they are much more likely to sign on.

When you are on television or radio, a dynamic, animated style can make the difference between an okay interview and one that is memorable.

Although everyone is nervous once a recording begins, keep these pointers in mind and practice them regularly. They can help you go from good to great and be considered a seasoned media pro:

* ❖ Pause and speed your speech. Think of yourself as a roller coaster rather than a freight train.
* ❖ Add volume and tempo. Variation—loud to soft, slow to fast—excites a listener's ear. Rapid speech is energizing. Slow, distinct language can also be effective, as it gives your statements weight and can help create a feeling of respect and admiration in your viewers or listeners. Again, balance is important, as is matching your personality style with your preferred speech patterns. A monotone is always deadly!
* ❖ Whispers work like a magnet, pulling the audience to you and to your point. Of course, whispering can only work if you have a good microphone.
* ❖ Practice with a digital recorder. Test out different speech techniques. Think of your favorite actors and how they might capture attention every time they are on screen because of their accenting, timing and overall speaking style.

SMART IDEA: Leaders prepare for intense Q&As.

You are in control during your formal presentation. You will not have to relinquish that control during the question and answer period if you have prepared for the inevitable difficult queries.

Follow this process ahead of any presentation:

1. Try to anticipate tough questions. Consider every possible concern that could prompt difficult queries.

2. Take a piece of paper and draw a vertical line down the middle. On the left side, list the negative issues; on the right, list positive points.

As you review the material in this format, find links from each negative issue on the left to something positive on the right. Then figure out how you can expand on the positive side of the issue to create an answer.

SMART IDEA: When speaking publicly, make good use of even poor audience questions.

Anyone who has spent time meeting with the media, investors, buyers or anyone else—either one-on-one or in a group—has experienced the frustration of poor participant questions at least once.

Imagine you have finished your presentation and asked if anyone has a question. Inevitably, someone asks something that shows he or she has not been listening. An insulting rejoinder is very tempting. But stop and ask yourself: would it be better to alienate your audience with a sharp retort or take a deep breath and answer the question politely? Consider also that other folks in the audience might similarly have missed the point.

Instead of getting frustrated, recognize that you have an opportunity and can use the moment to your advantage. In fact, you can use *any* question to reemphasize your main points.

The best way to open your response is: "That is a good question and goes back to the point I made earlier about…"

This saves face for the questioner and provides you with an opportunity to replay your message. A potential negative becomes a win/win thanks to your intelligent and generous attitude.

SMART IDEA: Get the bad news out of the way.

Certain issues might be consistently perceived as hurdles preventing investors from investing or hindering positive media coverage. If any aspect of your company has been deemed unattractive for any reason, consider changing your presentation strategy by starting with a frank assessment of the issues involved.

Yes, you read that correctly. Be bold and tell your audience what they won't like about your company! Nobody expects someone to stand up and say, "Let me tell you what you won't like about this deal." Doing so disarms the listener. They are no longer sitting and waiting to pounce because they believe you are going to try to hide the "ugly" stuff.

By using this direct approach, you will instead have likely earned a new level of trust, and your odds of having an engaging discussion will escalate exponentially.

SMART IDEA: Become an expert.

One of the most effective ways to successfully engage with the media through public relations is by positioning yourself as an expert in your field. There is a good deal of leeway in the media when it comes to experts. A designated company spokesperson, for example, is by definition an expert. Think about the topics you or others in your company can talk about with confidence and enthusiasm.

You can position yourself as an expert and reap the benefits of greater publicity for your company. In the early 1990s I appeared as an "expert" on every single daytime television talk show that filmed in New York City. I gave my opinion on relationships, nutritional issues and sex problems. I can assure you I am the leading expert in none of these fields. However, I was better at getting exposure than more erudite authorities. For every expert you see on TV, there are at least 10 others who probably know far more about the topic at hand; they just don't know how to get themselves interviewed. Some, of course, also don't want to be bothered. That's fine, but that attitude doesn't sell products, build a brand or raise a stock price.

Playboy's media department once mailed out packs of Rolodex cards to important media contacts. Each card in the pack was categorized by subject at the top, with the name and contact information for the specific *Playboy* editor who could serve as an expert in that area. Experts were offered in art, sports, music, movies, photography, books, fashion, travel and—no surprise—sex. This strategy, as you can imagine, generated countless media hits for the magazine's "experts" and helped brand *Playboy* in a variety of ways for years.

While we are on the topic of positioning yourself as an expert, let me tell you—from personal experience—that writing a book is one of the most effective strategies. Your name on a well-written book in your area of expertise, with a fresh perspective that is uniquely yours, offers major advantages. It positions you as an expert in your field. Your book can become the catalyst that attracts bigger and better placements and public speaking engagements. Most of all, it is a remarkably effective marketing tool that can open doors for you.

I can hear you now: "With my grueling schedule, how can I find time to write a book?" Or, "I'm not a writer." Or, "What exactly would I write about?" My response to all these protests is—Judy Katz. Judy, my dear friend and long-time colleague, is an extraordinarily talented book collaborator and book packager. After even a brief conversation, she can extract the "book in you," and provide you with the perfect trend-based perspective that will make your book stand out from anything currently available. Also, she can come up with a powerful title and subtitle almost immediately. I still don't know how she does it! Judy has perfected her proprietary "brain dump" strategy that allows her to ghostwrite your book in *your* voice. Her company, Ghostbooksters, can produce a beautifully written, professional book that you can proud of within a few months. Books are Judy's passion, so if you are interested, feel free to call her at 212.580.8833 or email her at judy@ghostbooksters.com. And tell her I told you to call!

When you let the media know you are available for interviews as an expert, be sure to send them a bio or C.V. and a background news release outlining your area of expertise. If you do have a book, offer that too, but don't send it until they request it to be sent. Don't be concerned if you don't get an immediate response to your offer—although you can call or email them once to ask if they received your material. One day, sooner or later, if you keep your name in front of the media, you *will* be called upon as an expert. A word of caution: doing "expert" interviews is actually lot of fun and can become habit-forming!

Imagine the potential coverage if you have the expertise and the right public relations "machine" continuously propelling you into the media! Position yourself as an expert and you'll multiply the chances of seeing your name in print—or seeing yourself on prime-time television.

SMART IDEA: Know your facts; make predictions.

An in-demand media expert not only knows the facts and can discuss them confidently, but is willing to predict what those facts mean for the near or distant future. Everybody makes guesses about what the future will bring. Experts are more courageous—they've learned the fundamental facts about a situation and make plausible predictions.

The courageous, interesting expert will be rewarded with media interest. If that is you, prepare to enjoy lots of free publicity. The downside is that, from time to time, your predictions will be wrong. Never mind. Throughout history, so-called experts have been making predictions that were occasionally incorrect. Didn't some authority figures once say the earth couldn't possibly be round? Or that no airplane would ever get off the ground? Or that nobody would listen to that talking box called a radio? I could make a list of experts who missed the boat as long as this book and then some. If we looked at the newspapers on Black Thursday, October 29, 1929, we'd probably find some pundit insisting that the market was perfectly sound.

The media exposure you get as an expert is usually well worth it. This means you will need to make time to develop strong sound bites. A good publicist can also help you with this. At my company, we help form these sound bites and news angles for our clients daily; we suggest thoughtful opinions, and help our clients sound authoritative. Again, don't spend too much time worrying about being proved wrong. If this happens, it will usually be long after you've made your prediction. People won't remember that so much as they will retain a positive impression, recalling that they saw you, heard you or read about you—ideally, all of the above.

The extensive free publicity I received as an "expert" helped me launch myself into many productive business relationships and, ultimately, led to my founding several of my companies. I have only the best memories of my years in front of the camera—now let's make it your turn!

SMART IDEA: Keep your publicity photo current.

Don't skimp in this area: take the time, spend a little bit more and have a good photo taken of yourself. I suggest you hire a professional photographer. Keep in mind the purpose of the picture is to enhance the reporter's story.

If you wear a suit all day, that's the best choice for attire. If you spend a significant portion of your time working in some other kind of clothing, you might consider having a few shots taken in that style as well. For example, if you work regularly with researchers in a laboratory, you might want to keep some shots handy with you in a lab coat.

It is equally important to have a photograph that is current. There are few things more awkward for my company than to have to break the news to a client that although their favorite photograph makes them look great, it doesn't look like them anymore, or shows them dressed in a long-outdated style. Reporters will ask for your photo almost every time they interview you. They might offer to send out a staff photographer for a story, but you can't count on this. Make sure you have a good photo of yourself that's no more than three years old. You change, styles change and you want to be viewed as a professional on top of the media game.

SMART IDEA: A quality video news release (VNR) reel will increase your odds of attracting national television and cable airtime.

When you have something significant to report, or you're at the head of an interesting trend and have the expertise, success stories and good visual elements to "show and tell" your story—a video of your news is an excellent way to reach mass audiences quickly and effectively. A well-produced, 45-second to three-minute video news release (VNR), with an extra few minutes of broadcast roll (B-roll), produced both with and without sound so that TV producers have extra footage to choose from, can be an essential component in attracting national exposure. Like any big breaking news story, a VNR that is widely picked up by the national media—and it does happen—can also help you become a household name.

VNRs need not be expensive to be effective. Producing a good VNR reel runs anywhere from $2,000 to $25,000 and up, depending on the complexity of the subject. This is an area where my company always provides its clients with multiple bids. Shop around and watch some of the vendor's previous VNRs. You might also include photographs, charts and other elements that can be incorporated into the reel. You want a professional, smooth-flowing reel that encapsulates your message and your company's products or services in a positive, entertaining and memorable way.

The primary goal of the VNR is to relay your message briefly. Producers who accept your VNR might choose not to air it in its entirety, so take control and make it short to begin with. The extra footage can be in the B-roll and can include more experts providing opinions, additional success stories and a silent scene shot at your business or another location. You will also need to provide a written script that narrates your VNR. The script allows each station's anchorperson or reporter to describe the VNR, although you should be aware that they often veer from your script to make their own comments. I have often found these independent comments to be even more favorable than what was written into the script.

Under the right circumstances, VNRs represent a winning formula. Your company gets the desired national exposure, and the television news station gets free and interesting news it can use.

SMART IDEA: Media events are overrated.

Yes, you read that correctly. Admittedly, this statement is not something you normally hear from someone in public relations! Some PR people make a lot of money coordinating special events that target the media, with lots of hours billed for arranging and staffing. Yet I've always doubted the return they provide for the company that pays for these events.

People often equate turnout with success. I don't. The "crowds" are often an illusion.

Big events, in my opinion, are often little more than a momentary ego-booster for the CEO. The crowds cheer—when they're not too busy eating or drinking their free refreshments—and tell him or her how great they are. However, press coverage is most often slim to none, and other benefits are usually hard to measure.

If something or someone deserves media attention, a well-written and well-disseminated press release, followed by the necessary follow-up telephone calls to reporters, will garner much more media attention than most large-scale media events.

Follow this advice and you'll save your company and its shareholders a small fortune that can be better spent on real results-oriented PR.

SMART IDEA: For flawless events, use a checklist of the basics. Then check your list not once or twice but as many times as necessary.

Checklists are essential to the success of any event. It is also vitally important to have a checklist for the media release announcing the event.

Use the following to make sure the news release about your event covers all possible details. Leave one out and you risk having spent a lot of money for a lackluster turnout.

Be sure the release:

- ❖ Has a headline that *sells* the event, not just describes it.
- ❖ Highlights the correct date, time and place.
- ❖ States clearly if the event is free. If there is a charge, make sure this is mentioned, along with any parking fee.
- ❖ Details how tickets can be obtained.
- ❖ Lists any registration or reservation deadlines.
- ❖ Spells all names correctly, including those of any sponsors.
- ❖ Mentions any food, beverages or hors d'oeuvres that will be served.
- ❖ Offers alternative plans in case of inclement weather.
- ❖ Explains how to obtain additional information and has all pertinent contact information in the body of the release.
- ❖ Lists a phone number that has a live person answering.
- ❖ Has been double-checked and triple-checked for accuracy of content, spelling and format.

CHAPTER 9:

Mastering the Art & Science of Being Interviewed

Smart executives pay attention, learn and practice the right ways of participating in interviews. Fielding questions from print or broadcast reporters demands a different set of skills than those required for public speaking or for writing news releases. When you are being interviewed, *you are not in charge* in the ways you might normally be accustomed. Yet as an interviewee, *you certainly do not have to give up control.*

Filtered through his or her own sensibilities and perceptions, the interviewer gets to communicate your message to the groups he or she wants to reach within the public-at-large. This acknowledged, you can still play a major part in shaping the story that is told. In this chapter, you'll learn how a savvy interviewee can make a big difference in the ways the media portray his or her company to the public-at-large, which will include grabbing the attention of investors, if desired.

SMART IDEA: Your goals for any interview must be clearly defined—in writing—prior to the interview.

Before agreeing to do an interview, an experienced interviewee tabulates three or four main points they want to make during the filming.

In writing these all-important notes of what you want to convey to the interviewer, begin with the most important point and work your way through a brief list. Then memorize it. I am a big believer in outlines. Everyone has stage fright, and even actors forget their lines—what they call "going up." Identify your core messages and practice saying them in different ways.

You should also have an agenda, just as you would for any important business meeting. Do your best to cover your key message points completely before your allotted time is up.

One last thing: expect that a reporter will have his or her own agenda for the interview. Don't forget to be prepared for any kind of question that might be thrown at you. Anticipate the "tough" questions. Prepare answers ahead of time. If you fail to do so, you might wind up struggling for an answer and looking like a deer caught in headlights.

SMART IDEA: Your actions and words must always serve to sustain the faith and trust of your employees, clients and current or potential investors.

David S. Pottruck, former president and CEO of Charles Schwab, in his book *Clicks and Mortar* (Jossey-Bass, 2001), recalls answering a reporter's question with a witty remark. At the moment he was making that remark and listening to the laughter it drew, he suddenly pictured his words as a headline in the national news…and it was definitely *not* a headline he would ever want to be associated with.

Pottruck thought quickly and acted immediately. He expanded on his initial response to the question more thoroughly than he ordinarily would have. Then he looked for the reporter and stated clearly that he never should have made the remark, that it could be misconstrued and that, taken out of context, he now realized, it certainly wouldn't appear witty. Fortunately, the reporter graciously agreed that it was not necessary to print the quip.

Not everyone is so lucky. If you make an ill-considered, offbeat quip, it can easily make it into print or be reported on TV. As a leader of your company and as its public face, your actions and words must always serve to maintain the faith and trust of the people who listen to you and perhaps put their hard-earned money into buying your stock. Sometimes silence is golden. What might be acceptable for someone else in your organization to say or do might not be equally appropriate for you.

Always ask yourself these two questions:

❖ Could my statement(s) or my explanation be interpreted by an employee, associate, partner, customer, investor or the media in a way that would shake their faith in my leadership?

❖ Could my statement(s) be misinterpreted and held against my company or me?

Words are more potent than you might realize. In media interviews, and in life, choose your words carefully. If you use them wisely, they will serve you well.

SMART IDEA: Ask key questions before agreeing to an interview.

Whether you are the one who is going to be interviewed, or you are setting up the interview for someone else in the company, there are a few questions you need to ask in advance:

1. What day and time—including time zone—is the interview?

2. Where will the interview be held?

3. How long will the interview be?

4. Does the reporter have a specific agenda for the interview? If so, what is the proposed content or nature of the conversation? What will you and he/she talk about?

If you or your public relations agency did not initiate the interview, try to obtain as much information as possible about the reporter's motives by asking some subtle but incisive questions. You want to appear unsurprised that the media are interested in you or your company, but you also want to be prepared. Thus, you will want to find out:

1. Who will be doing the interview?

2. Will others be interviewed on the same topic? If so, who?

3. Is the reporter hoping to create controversy with multiple interviews of people with opposing views, or is he/she trying to build on one particular angle or   point of view (POV)? Will the story be slanted in any particular direction? Try to find out that direction.

4. Can a list of questions be obtained in advance? (Be prepared not to get it).

5. If radio, cable or television: Will the interview be live or taped, and will it be edited? Will there be a studio audience? Will questions come only from the interviewer or from the audience as well? Will there be telephone call-ins?

6. For television interviews: Can I provide B-roll? This is a broadcast reel that you supply. It can have sound with the visuals, but most often is silent footage of a laboratory, manufacturing plant, street scene or other relevant background to make your completed interview more interesting. Also ask if you can use charts or photographs, or bring product samples to show on air. You also want to know if *they* will add any pre-taped content. If so, you should ask to view it prior to the taping.

7. What, if anything, other than the above, should I bring with me?

8. Can I bring an associate or friend? They seldom object, especially if that person is your publicist. While you are on air, your guest will most likely sit in the "green room" where they can watch you being interviewed on a monitor. They can usually enjoy coffee, tea, soda and a muffin, doughnut or bagel—the typical green room fare. You will also have to wait your turn there, so you too can enjoy a complimentary treat, too. I recommend limiting your coffee consumption before an interview. It can cause jitters or sweats, making you uncomfortable and impairing the smooth flow of your speech.

Asking questions ahead of time can eliminate serious discomfort later on. Don't worry about whether you sound professional. There are no stupid questions, especially when you are facing a new experience. Pros ask questions. A good PR professional would never allow a client to do an interview "blind." There might be times when it pays to be reticent, but this is not one of them. If you've been called out of the blue to do an interview, you need to find out as much as you can. As my best friend's grandmother always said, "If you don't ask, darling, you don't get." Ask those critical questions!

SMART IDEA: Consider practicing with a media professional prior to any television interview.

This is a smart idea I wish I had known before my own early television appearances. Practicing with a pro would have shown me that I sometimes speak out of the side of my mouth, which looks quite odd when aired. My other early classic error was that when I was speaking, I tended to move my shoulders up and down like a jackhammer. Needless to say, in close-ups this looked pretty ridiculous. It looked like I was warming up for an aerobics class, not appearing on TV as an expert commentator.

Maybe you have no such idiosyncrasies. But, then again, maybe you do. Maybe you have a verbal tic, such as tagging "you know" onto every other sentence or inappropriately using the word "like." Maybe you make noises like "umm" while you're thinking, or unconsciously play with your hair, lick your lips or cough. These nervous habits—what gamblers call "tells"—can be quite annoying to the listening or viewing audience. A pro could help uncover and correct such things before you have to endure a chuckle, or worse, at your expense.

Here's a checklist of dos and don'ts for interviews:

The Basics:

❖ Arrive early with appropriate photo ID or you won't get into the building/studio.

❖ No cocktails prior to interviews—regardless of how you think they might help you relax. Be yourself—that will be just fine. Watch the coffee too, especially on an empty stomach.

❖ Bring some face powder that matches your natural complexion, and a brush—not a sponge or puff. Wipe down your face and fluff on some powder to keep your gleam to a minimum. This advice is not only for women; it applies to men too. The big shows have makeup artists—the smaller ones usually do not. Find this out as well. Sweating while you're speaking will undermine your credibility. And you *will* sweat—at least when the hot stage lights come on!

❖ Be aware of time. Television news interviews are typically about three minutes. The time passes wickedly fast. Remember you've got a lot of ground to cover and you need to be concise—these are your three minutes of fame.

❖ Do not bring notes on the air with you—you will look amateurish.

Speaking:

❖ Stick to your three or four key messages.

❖ Keep your comments brief. Remember, there's a reason you are called "the guest." The interviewer is "the star." If you let him or her be the "star" interviewer, they will likely help you shine too.

❖ Watch trade jargon. The general public is watching. For maximum publicity results, everyone needs to know what you are talking about—not just the medical or scientific professional or the technically astute. Talk in plain English to the whole world.

❖ Skip the wisecracks and sarcasm unless you are a professional comedian. The risk is too great that you will misfire.

❖ Never tell a lie.

Body Language:

❖ Again, try to pinpoint and avoid any nervous mannerisms.

❖ Sit up straight. Don't slouch. (Am I starting to sound like your mother?)

❖ Engage the interviewer with direct eye contact. If there's a live audience, also look out at them occasionally. It's okay to let them know you know they're there!

❖ Genuine emotion is good as long as it doesn't become excessive. This could even include tears—at the appropriate moment. Presidents, champion athletes and plenty of others have had their moments on camera with teary eyes.

❖ Don't assume you can "play to the camera." Most shows are filmed with two or three cameras. I assure you that you won't have any idea which one the producer is going to switch to at any given moment. Unless it's a satellite interview and you are told to look directly into the camera, look at your interviewer.

Pitfalls to Avoid During the Interview:

❖ Avoid getting defensive or angry. If you find your blood pressure rising, take a deep breath. Then start making whatever points you want to make. Study politicians who usually master this trick early on, and know how to take *any* question and turn it to their advantage. Study how an oft-quoted politician makes the points he wants, no matter what the question asked. Practice politely responding to objectionable questions with "Excellent question" or "I am so glad you asked me that question, (interviewer's name)." Then talk about one of your three primary interview points.

❖ Reporters are skilled at making incorrect statements simply to elicit a reaction. "Leading questions" are a perfect example. Listen carefully and, if necessary, correct any misstatements made by the interviewer; any misstatements the interviewer attributed to you; or a misstatement about you or your company made by any other guest. It is perfectly okay, in fact mandatory, to correct an error rather than let it go unchallenged. If you can provide hard evidence such as statistics, studies or surveys to support any claims you are making, do so.

❖ Stay focused. Expect distractions and don't allow them to throw you.

❖ Stay "on message" and composed at all times. Also, don't assume the interview is over until you hear "cut." This goes for any form of broadcast, including radio.

One of the most important points to emphasize is this: it is all right not to have all the answers to the questions you might be asked. The important thing is to have a good response ready, such as:

"I don't have enough information to answer that right now."
"I think someone else might be more suitable to answer that."
"I'm not sure I'm qualified to answer that."

Answers like these make you look professional rather than evasive. Admitting what you don't know often enhances one's credibility. Mark this page and use it as a reminder before you do any interview.

SMART IDEA: Follow these dress code guidelines or consult a wardrobe professional prior to a television/cable interview.

I have done a tremendous number of both taped and live television interviews and I learned the hard way how to dress for these occasions.

I made some mortifying wardrobe errors in my first few interviews that even the station's makeup and wardrobe people couldn't cover up. In some cases, I was quite surprised when I was asked back for another interview.

Some of what I learned might help you think about *your* interviews in a new way.

When I am nervous—and I confess I still am every time I do any kind of public speaking, whether teaching or being interviewed on television—I sweat. To make matters worse, I also tend to break out in blotchy red hives down my neck and across my chest. After finding out that Mick Jagger of the Rolling Stones also says he still gets nervous before any performance 50 years into the game, I now consider my physical responses a minor annoyance. Instead, I now look at these responses as indications that adrenaline is propelling me into high gear for maximum effectiveness during my appearance.

Nonetheless, knowing in advance what can occur requires a few compensatory modifications. Here I share what I learned the hard way:

❖ Don't wear a silk blouse or shirt without a jacket. If you sweat like I do, silk shows it big-time!

❖ High necklines for ladies are more appropriate than scoop necks—no cleavage.

❖ Classic pinstripe suits are fine. Otherwise, lose the stripes and checks.

❖ Avoid blouses, dresses or shirts with bold patterns. You want the attention on *you*, not your outfit.

❖ No distracting ties.

❖ Go easy on conspicuous accessories or jewelry—unless that's what you're selling. Your face and what you have to say should be the focal point of the interview, not your accessories.

❖ Loud colors are also a no-no. Hint: most shades of blue tend to look best on television.

❖ Don't wear a black suit and white shirt. The contrast makes balancing light while recording more challenging and will make you look a sallow, nasty shade of reddish-yellow.

❖ Make sure your shirt is a classic style. No extra-large collars or shirts that are darker than your suit. Otherwise you might make a negative impression that will be difficult to dispel.

❖ Classically styled suits are also the best bet for both men and women. Don't go "high-fashion"—unless you're in the fashion business. Remember, you want to appear as the consummate business professional, and what is fashionable in one area of the country—or world—might be quite unfashionable in another.

❖ When in doubt, bring one or two additional wardrobe options with you, and ask the producer or your smart publicist to help you choose.

Even if you are in a more casual business—for example, if you are the CEO of a chain of auto parts stores—and typically dress informally, a suit is still your best option for interviews unless the producer requests otherwise. A well-tailored, classic suit will always make you look sharp and businesslike. Casual clothes can send a message to viewers that might block the impression of competency you seek to convey.

SMART IDEA: Radio interviews are an easy and effective way to get media coverage.

Radio is one of the greatest untapped opportunities in public relations. Radio offers a huge outreach to attentive, loyal listeners who are often "captive," such as those stuck in traffic on their way to or from work. It's relatively easy to get radio coverage. As a bonus, radio drastically reduces your wardrobe and bad-hair-day worries, plus you never have to leave your office.

When you do a radio interview, remember to give a simple, easy-to-re-member website address or phone number for more information. "Easy-to-remember" is the key term here, as many of those listening to your interview might not have a pen or pencil handy.

SMART IDEA: To gain maximum benefit from a Satellite Media Tour, tie the company's interview to a newsworthy event.

The Satellite Media Tour (SMT) has long been used successfully by politicians, celebrities promoting a new movie or book, and smart public relations officers of publicly traded companies. The SMT is a series of pre-booked interviews with national and/or local television or radio stations. These interviews are typically arranged a month or more prior to an event. The person could be interviewed in a TV studio or, in the case of radio, almost anywhere with access to a landline. The interviews are generally brief, lasting three to seven minutes, but some can go for 15 minutes or even half an hour. The process includes booking and conducting the interviews and tracking the results.

Fees for a SMT range from an average of $8,000 and up for a radio satellite tour to anywhere from $18,000 to $80,000 for a national satellite television tour. SMTs are expensive—but cost-effective when you con-sider travel costs and time saved to reach targeted audiences.

For success, provide key media outlets with a great story headline, an introduction and a series of suggested questions. This kind of preparation increases the credibility of the story during the booking phase and keeps the media interested because if they know the story better, they are better prepared to ask the right questions.

The day of the tour involves a visit to a predetermined television studio that offers satellite capabilities. At these studios, there is a pre-arranged linkup to a satellite. Providing some B-roll or additional film footage can lead to slightly longer and visually interesting segments. A rehearsal should be held the day before the event. You know by now how much I believe in the adage, "Practice makes perfect!"

Results from this kind of media exposure can be measured immediately upon airing. You can also hire a company that specializes in tracking such media events. These companies, such as Video Monitoring Services (VMS), sell recordings they've tracked, complete with any "intro" or "trailer" run on the TV program. Purchasing these professionally produced recordings of your interviews and creating a reel is critical for future use in attracting other media outlets to interview you. A producer might ask to see prior on-air experience before booking you as an expert. The recordings you collect from your SMT should provide plenty of documentation that you are an effective guest. This footage can also be useful as a reel to loop at your trade show booth, annual meetings and elsewhere.

If you've got the budget and a newsworthy angle, well-planned SMTs can make a priceless contribution to your company's overall public relations plan.

SMART IDEA: You don't have to give a "better" answer.

Investors, fund managers, analysts and reporters looking for a unique edge often ask the same question more than once during an interview. This can grate on your nerves. It's comparable to a child nagging their parents by repeating the same question until they get what they want. In the process, the question might be tweaked, but the investor or reporter is usually digging for a particular answer—and like a child, won't quit until they get it.

You never need to come up with a better response than the one you gave—or chose not to give—earlier in the interview. The only time to revisit a question is when it's in your best interests to do so, and when you believe you really do have a better answer or because you want to reemphasize your point.

Do not cave to pressure and feel compelled to provide a whole new answer. Likely this will only complicate things, as you might start to dig a hole that could cave in on you later. Listen to the questions carefully. Make sure they are questions—and *not* statements—from the reporter. Stay focused on your message points. Establishing and maintaining personal control is critical to the entire interview.

When asked the same question more than once, feel free to repeat your original comment verbatim. Or simply say with a smile: "I believe I've answered that question already."

Remember: a reporter's job—just like that of a good investment manager or analyst—is to unearth whatever they can that might not already be known by the general public. That's what they get paid to do. If they can manipulate you or wear you down for a better story, they will try to do so. Respect that they are doing their job to the best of their abilities. At the same time, recognize that *your* job is to share information with public audiences when you are ready—*not* because of pressure from a skilled reporter or financial professional.

SMART IDEA: Don't feel compelled to fill any silent gaps during an interview.

One of the biggest mistakes made by inexperienced interviewees is to not know when to keep quiet. If there is a silent moment, it is not your job to fill it.

Silence can serve a twofold purpose. First, it might allow a reporter to collect his or her thoughts. Second, it might be an interviewing tactic designed to provoke you to say more than you might have said otherwise. Reporters are experts at luring their subjects into feeling obligated to speak up in order to break the silence. Like a fisherman who can wait quietly for hours waiting for the big fish to bite, they are patiently hoping that you, too, will "bite" and say something you did not intend to reveal.

Enjoy the silence. Use it to collect your thoughts. Don't feel compelled to fill the void. It isn't necessary, and such impulses can prove a disadvantage to you and the overall interview.

During an on-air interview, if you really want to fill the silence, try this. Using your best acting skills, pretend that another great thought just popped into your mind and say: "What I really think is important for your viewers to hear is…" and bring out another arrow from your arsenal of message points.

SMART IDEA: From the minute any interview starts until it sees print or airtime, every word you say is "for the record," which means "for publication."

Any interview you do is not over until you have parted or hung up the phone. Taking this rule a step further, no interview is truly over until it is in print or hits the airwaves. Never forget this, regardless of any body language or actions that might mistakenly lead you to believe otherwise.

The quickest way to ensure that your candid asides see print is to offer the reporter a comment that is "not for publication."

If you are shortsighted or inexperienced enough to make such a comment, you deserve the consequences. This is good old common sense—which is unfortunately not always so common. If you step into a lion's cage, don't be surprised if you get clawed. When dealing with reporters, remember that their job is to write exciting stories. Telling them "secrets" will only trigger their natural urge to "kiss and tell"—no matter what they might promise you.

You might feel a reporter is your friend, but that friendship does not extend to babysitting you. A reporter's only objective is to "get the story."

More to the point, their job is to deliver a *compelling* story: translate "compelling" as "controversial" and you'll get a better picture of the game. Anticipate that a reporter will skillfully lull you into a comfortable conversation to get you to lower your guard. They'll be doing this during interviews with your competitors, too, who also are likely being interviewed for any significant sector or issue story.

A good adage to keep in mind is this: if you want a guarantee that a story will be 100 percent positive about you or your company, take out an ad. Otherwise, study these ideas, use them to your advantage and enjoy the free press.

SMART IDEA: You will never get the last word with the media.

When you are angry about anything and about to be interviewed, make sure you calm down before speaking with the reporter. Passion about your subject is one thing—anger during any interview is another.

If a reporter helps contribute to your anger, take a deep breath, count to 10 if you must, and think carefully about the pleasant, direct answer you are about to give.

Becoming angry with a reporter and acting on it is a luxury you cannot afford. Your mistaken belief that you are going to have the "last word" only proves your media naiveté.

Reporters go to press every day. Rest assured, on any controversial topic, a reporter will have the last word, and their opinion will be what appears in print or on tape for the entire world to read or see!

CHAPTER 10:

Critical Issues to Weigh When Dealing with a Crisis

Financial regulators and business reporters are working day and night to uncover corporate scandals and missteps. The spotlight is on the structures of corporate governance, and on accountability and transparency in financial reporting. The Sarbanes-Oxley Act and other regulations highlight the need for strict corporate governance, and represent a glaring and harsh new spotlight focused on companies if they do not follow these regulations properly. Publicly traded companies need to be keenly aware of how these regulations affect them. Management teams need to be prepared to answer the same question that investors from Main Street to Wall Street are asking of every listed corporation: "Is this a company I can trust?"

None of us wants to be in an accident—and smart people wear safety belts. You might be absolutely convinced that your company is doing business honestly and forthrightly, and you might still run into problems. Certain problems that arise are outside the control of even the best management teams, but others can be avoided. Smart crisis management strategically reviews potential challenges while outlining a plan so you are ready to cope with whatever might come along. Here is a selection of ideas to help you before, during and after a crisis.

SMART IDEA: You must be constantly aware of what could constitute a crisis for your company.

Dishonest executives and fraudulent finances are only the most obvious examples of what might precipitate a crisis for a given company. Lawsuits from shareholders, consumers and customers are other potential challenges. Then there are law firms that "troll" by launching investigations into whatever they deem investigation-worthy—however unfounded and potentially detrimental to shareholders. Certainly, the plaintiffs' bar has become much more active. These might seem like extreme examples. Yet as one securities litigator noted: "It is totally implausible that any significant company is not sued in any calendar year for something." Even one lawsuit can tarnish the reputation of a company and directly affect its share price. There is often little difference between the court of public opinion and the court of law.

Crises occur, and most often fall into these categories:

❖ Poor financial performance
❖ Product liabilities/recalls
❖ Disasters and accidents
❖ Regulatory issues
❖ Environmental problems

❖ Dissatisfaction with the company by employees, shareholders, consumers or others.

Company leaders and their representatives must be constantly aware of what could constitute a crisis. Here are some basic questions you need to be able to answer, particularly if there was a crisis at some point in your company's past:

❖ What kinds of issues do we or might we have that could be considered fuel for a crisis?

❖ How could we have improved our actions in regards to crises we might have dealt with in the past?

When you ask yourselves these questions, you should reflect on whether:

❖ There was (or is) internal confusion in your company.

❖ The vetting system was (or is) in place.

❖ The chain of command functioned (and is functioning) properly.

❖ The spokesperson was (and is) well-trained.

❖ The CEO was (and is) appropriately involved.

❖ The company came off (and comes off) as arrogant or unfeeling.

❖ The response was (and will be) fast or slow and accurate or misleading.

SMART IDEA: Have a crisis plan of action in place *before* the crisis.

To be fully prepared to handle a possible crisis, and to make sure that any previous bad experiences do not recur, intelligent, advanced organization is key. What follows is the crisis plan we have developed at my company, Dian Griesel Int'l. (DGI), for our clients:

❖ First, adjust your mindset. Hope for the best and prepare for the worst. What should help you sleep more soundly at night is having a crisis communications plan in place, one that includes notification and action steps to take at your local branches, if any, and at your headquarters. Set up a rapid response team, one that can be assembled and spring into action at a moment's notice.

❖ Create a notification process for your internal communications systems.

❖ Be conscious of media cycles. Time zone differences are never an excuse to avoid dealing promptly with inquiries from media or from other important parties. It's best to identify and empower a spokesperson for the company, both in the United States and overseas if you have offices in other countries. If you choose to not do this, make sure a "reliable source" is available night and day at your corporate headquarters.

❖ Identify who your third-party endorsers will be in the event of challenging events or attacks. These endorsers are friendly sources that you can offer to the media. If you come under attack, these respected, credible individuals should be on standby, ready to say good things about your company and your management. They can be a critical weapon in your public relations defense arsenal.

❖ Identify the top 10 or 15 people you will need to notify in order to be proactive in getting out your side of a story. This should ideally be a balanced combination of industry or trade analysts, credentialed supporters, and contacts at local, regional and national media as well as select trades and others.

❖ Make sure your legal and communications people get together or contact each other regularly to go over vulnerable issues so that no one on your team is ever caught off-guard.

Put together a crisis policy manual for your company that covers all of the above. When new executives assume leadership positions, the policies should be reviewed by and with them so that they too are never caught off-guard.

SMART IDEA: In the face of a crisis, take charge by acknowledging the problem.

When facing a crisis, take charge quickly by acknowledging the problem. This does not mean taking the blame. Under all circumstances, your immediate response and focus must be about solutions, not about assigning blame.

We are living in an era of instant communication and news travels quickly. We'll delve into this more deeply in Part II of this book. But for now, suffice it to say, if the CEO is not on top of the crisis and responding in the moment, he or she will no longer be considered the leading source of information. This places your company in an unnecessarily defensive position.

Here are some rules of crisis management that should not be overlooked:

❖ Act quickly, thoughtfully and honestly. The buck stops with you. Assure your investing public that somebody is concerned about the problem, and that "somebody" is *you*. Openly take responsibility for resolving the crisis.

❖ Understand that you are going to have to explain things. Keep your staff informed, but allow only a designated spokesperson, in addition to yourself, the right to speak for the company and answer public questions.

❖ Gather all the facts. Base your responses to the media and to the investing public strictly on those facts.

❖ Consult a communications specialist—one whom you know is adept at handling crises.

❖ Act effectively. Make sure you reinforce that you are on top of the situation every step of the way.

❖ Act consistently. Plan each move you make, and ensure your actions are congruent with your overall message regarding the crisis.

❖ Have everyone on board. Make sure all your employees—from your top executives and middle managers to support staff—know you are going to weather the storm and how you plan to do it.

❖ Stand tall. Don't play the ostrich and hide your head in the sand. If you do, the bad news will still be there when you stick your head out—and might be even worse because of the time lost. If you are aware of bad news, be the one to announce it. You shouldn't allow yourself to be placed in a position where you are reacting to damaging information revealed by outside parties. This seriously hurts management's credibility like nothing else.

❖ Accept the role of the media and do not view or treat the press as the enemy. In crisis situations, the media can actually help you. In a crisis, most companies experience immobilizing fear and do the worst thing possible: issue a classic "no comment." This tends to make people think the worst and can only hurt you. Give the media confirmed facts. Again, you do not have to have a ready answer to every question. Assure the reporter that the company is on top of the situation and working to resolve the problem.

A crisis can go either way depending on how you respond to it. If improperly handled, it can spell the beginning of the end for a company. If properly handled, it can be the impetus for necessary changes and effective progress. Whether or not you recognize it, the investing public and media are more concerned with your reaction than with the ultimate solution.

One last thought on handling a crisis: don't try to blame somebody else or claim the crisis wasn't your fault. A denial and attempt at diversion makes management look ineffectual and casts doubt on the company's ethics. One only has to look at the skillful way Johnson & Johnson handled its Tylenol crisis more than two decades ago, compared to how the global accounting firm Arthur Andersen handled its scandal involving Enron and WorldCom. Today, one company is thriving; the other no longer exists.

SMART IDEA: Maintain credibility by highlighting key issues.

I can't stress this strongly enough: do not attempt to hide your bad news in the body of a press release. This is a common mistake, and although the tactic might have worked once or twice in the past, it doesn't work anymore. All it will do is hurt your reputation. Credibility is vital for the survival and profitability of any company. Maintain yours, and you will ultimately build and enjoy a strong and supportive shareholder base.

The good news is that bad news is fleeting.

The benefit of living in our short-attention-span society is that if you've been shamed or maligned in a media story, you will most likely remember it much longer than anyone else. Those who were gored by the bull remember the pain of the incident, while others have already moved on.

If you don't like what you're reading or hearing in the press about yourself or your company, do whatever you can do to change the situation wisely and unemotionally, but remember that tomorrow there will be another set of headlines.

SMART IDEA: Neither corporate management nor highly trained accountants can hide behind—or even rely upon—the restatement option.

According to *Compliance Week*, the overall number of restatements filed by public companies fell in 2012, but the largest U.S. companies registered a second year of increases. Among restatements in 2012, the largest number, or 15 percent, were filed because of problems with debt, quasi-debt, warrants and equity security issues. The next largest batch, or 14.6 percent, arose because of problems with tax issues. Cash flow statement classification errors accounted for the third most common cause of restatements. Revenue recognition came in fourth on the list of problems.

There are times when restatements must be made, due to varied interpretation possibilities stemming from the ever-changing accounting environment laden with rules and regulations. However, as an all-purpose safety net for corporate finance departments, the damage can be heavy when a restatement is issued.

Shareholders are beginning to scrutinize restatements closely. To maintain your shareholder loyalty and continue to build and grow your company, make sure restatements are not a regular feature of your corporate communications plan! This is a case where once is more than enough, and twice might be a career-ender—or even kill off a company.

SMART IDEA: Avoid a fortress mentality when dealing with the media.

If you treat the media as the enemy, and build a figurative wall around yourself or your company for insulation and protection, those around you will assume you are ready for war. If you build walls to keep the media out, don't be surprised if they become somewhat hostile when they finally do break through—and they will. Repeated hostility toward the people who report the news means you won't have any friends left in the media when you need them the most. Not a good state of affairs!

Do not take media confrontations personally. You have a job to do, and so does the reporter who contacts you. Try to keep differences and conflicts at a professional level. The one who draws "first blood" by making the discussion personal also makes the situation more difficult. The resulting standoff will be much harder to resolve in a way that will prove satisfactory to you.

If a reporter has ever wronged you, and the issue is important enough to you, you have the option of taking your case public. Tell your side of the story to the publisher, to other reporters, to people who read your website, to readers of your advertising, newsletters, emails and to your own personnel. However, this is a drastic step that should never be taken lightly or without considerable deliberation. Above all, you don't want to give the impression of whining, of self-pity or any other less-than-powerful stance. You have a right to defend yourself and your company. However, before proceeding, please carefully consider the adage, "Never pick a fight with someone who buys ink by the barrel." The power of the press is not to be taken lightly.

SMART IDEA: Admit your mistakes, following prescribed techniques.

In an *Investor's Business Daily* column a while back—I cut it out to save it, but neglected to record the date—journalist Morey Stettner offered two pointers that can help if you ever need to publicly admit a mistake.

The first, Stettner says, is to apologize in terms of "past-present-future." Frame your action as something done in the past that you now recognize to be wrong. Promise never to do it again—a *present* solution. Then go into the future with an agenda that shows you intend to win back your shareholders' trust.

The second pointer is: when only regrets are called for, there is no need to apologize. Reserve "I'm sorry" for actions that were willfully wrong or intentionally deceiving. You certainly want to express regrets for honest mistakes and inadvertent errors. For example, suppose you made a decision that was ultimately so bad you had to reverse it. If it turns out the decision was made based on your reliance on wrong information, the proper statement is: "I made a mistake and I regret that. And this is how we are going to remedy the situation…"

SMART IDEA: "No comment" is an open invitation to publish a hostile story about you or your company.

"No comment" means you are not the person in charge. And that isn't the case, is it? As the head of your company, you *are* the person in charge. The rule here, taken the other way around, is that the person in charge must *always* have a comment.

That comment might be that you are:

❖ assessing the situation

❖ gathering the facts

❖ coordinating your team

❖ preparing a formal statement

To be perceived as a leader—and you do want that, always—you must have a comment.

Also, when confronted by a camera crew, never ask if the camera can be turned off when you speak to the interviewer. Even if they do turn the camera off, this is never a safe way to communicate because if they hear you, they can report on what they heard. Be careful! The best advice is, never make a comment you don't want to see in print or on TV.

As anyone with media experience can tell you, regardless of what the camera crew says, you have no idea what is actually being filmed *or* edited out. Asking if the camera can be turned off is like the "off the record" conversation you think you can have with a reporter. If the reporter or camera crew thinks your emotional breakdown will make good footage, you can be sure—regardless of what is said—that the tape is rolling. Smart camerapeople *never* turn off their cameras, so don't be naïve and expect them to, just because you asked nicely.

You might want to stand up for your rights. This can work against you as well. Legally, you do not have to talk to the media. At the same time, the media can legally quote other people on the record as well as off the record. When you pit yourself against the media, you're likely to come out bruised and bloody—since the media represent the public's "right to know." Ask some celebrities about their experiences with paparazzi and you will hear about the dark side of fame and fortune.

Of course, none of this will ever happen to you, because you will have followed the advice in *Engage*.

PART II:

Social Media: The Game Changer

In Part II, we explore how many of the smart ideas presented in Part I are applied in light of the power of the Internet. The Internet has changed the dissemination of the message and the speed of its delivery. I focus on the smart ideas that must be implemented to reap the benefits of the web and social media.

CHAPTER 11:

Making "Friends"
Through the Internet

social: of or relating to human society, the interaction of the individual and the group, or the welfare of human beings as members of society

media: the main means of mass communication regarded collectively

The Internet is a vast universe to which people worldwide contribute. It presents seemingly unlimited potential for obtaining information. Most people now get their news online. They also research potential purchases and partnerships online. It's big, and only getting bigger.

Whatever your feelings toward the Internet and/or the impact of social media, the sooner you understand and embrace its relevance and potential, the faster you will be able to open doors for your business. Many doors. Unlimited doors.

Consider not only *how* you heard about recent and significant news—but also how quickly you heard it. Odds are it was within minutes, if not seconds, after the event. Most likely, your opinion of the event was *instantly* and *emotionally* formed. You might or might not have opted to dig deeper, in search of more facts or coverage of the story by turning on the television or radio, picking up a newspaper or using a search engine or Twitter to find more stories surrounding the topic.

The Internet's power is largely free for the taking. One or more on-line outlets could be feeding you customers, partners and other desired affiliates.

Or those same outlets could be helping your enemies build their takeover of your business and the destruction of your reputation and brand, simply because they are more savvy and cognizant of the ideas within these pages.

It's been said that all is fair in love and war. There are no rules for attacks, they aren't fair, are rarely accurate and there are no good reasons required to start a "war." But be assured: attackers are out there and they are just waiting for their moment to pounce. Potentially worse, they almost always strike first with determination to ruin your name, sabotage your reputation and harm or derail your business.

The best defense is a strong offense.

Offensive marketing and public relations strategies must place laser focus on how to use the countless Internet forums, channels, social media networks and news feeds to fuel your business. It takes some work, but the good news is you don't have to be everywhere—just where it counts and where it is relevant to you and your business objectives.

You'll need a plan. It can start very simply, but will require time and energy for consistent execution. Then you can add to your plan, amend it, evolve it and build upon it—while maintaining its core.

Examine How Other Companies Are Maximizing the Internet

To stir your imagination, here are a few of the ways some well-known brands capitalized by taking their message to the web:

- ❖ Chilean wines profited as bloggers touted this next top "undiscovered" region.

- ❖ By launching five different Facebook pages, including OPEN Forum and Small Business Saturday, American Express gained new clients and free media coverage.

- ❖ NeuroMetrix, Inc. and Boston Therapeutics, Inc., two companies focused on serving the needs of people with diabetes, reached out to influential bloggers offering interviews.

- ❖ Offering free tickets to the largest U.S. gaming expo, Kmart built unlikely bridges between corporate America and video-gaming bloggers.

- ❖ Applied DNA Sciences, Inc. used online content and newsletters to educate consumers and corporate America about the unique identifying properties of DNA to combat production of counterfeit goods.

- ❖ Marley Coffee reinforced the ethical interests of its brand through a variety of online conversations, Instagram posts and articles with titles showcasing its creative brand names, including Lively Up, One Love and Simmer Down.

- ❖ The authors of *TurboCharged*® highlighted the success of dieting Facebook fans to make their book a #1 bestseller under every health category ranked by Amazon and the #26 bestseller of all books sold worldwide. The posts also led to a segment on *The Today Show.*

- ❖ Intellicheck Mobilisa, Inc.'s barZapp™ rose to the top of the business app lists within 30 days due to content marketing with feature stories widely disseminated across the Internet that discussed new ways to detect fake IDs.

❖ Con Edison used social media in smart and diligent ways during Hurricane Irene to keep New Yorkers informed.

❖ Charles & Colvard, Ltd. enhanced its online sales via a series of widely disseminated, free-for-use articles that shared educational information about buying precious, ethically created gems.

❖ The "GEICO Gecko Journey Across America" Naked Cowboy YouTube video hit earned 7,000 views in hours thanks to a Twitter push.

❖ San Diego Gas & Electric used Twitter when the power went out to keep its customers informed.

❖ Harvard Apparatus Regenerative Technology, Inc. advanced the understanding of regenerative medicine in online articles that shed light on the entire industry sector—not just itself. These and other PR strategies resulted in a two-hour Meredith Vieira special for NBC-TV.

❖ A community bank created a few mobile apps and began a sponsored story campaign, resulting in five percent of the community liking its Facebook page.

❖ In the burgeoning sweetener market, Stevia First Corp. gained thought leadership positioning by accepting interviews with online bloggers and traditional media alike, as well as posting lots of "sweet" information on its website.

❖ Caliber Imaging & Diagnostics touted noninvasive testing for beauty marks vs. melanomas while featuring famous redheads in online articles on St. Patrick's Day. Creativity kept its VivaScope® device in thousands of articles in print and online outlets.

❖ Farmers Insurance agents sold 200 policies through a Facebook "Agents Page" after a FarmVille social gaming campaign gained more than 31,000 fans in two weeks.

❖ Alliqua Biomedical created content educating medical professionals and the general population on proper wound care. Nurses across the country engaged in the conversation with the company about their favorite features of the Company's wound care products.

❖ Harvard Bioscience, Inc. shared online articles on ways to make labs more efficient, which in turn helped direct new customers to its extensive equipment catalogs.

❖ Citi focused marketing energies on female earners by creating a first-of-its-kind LinkedIn community for professional women that grew to more than 100,000 members in nine months.

❖ The ALS Association created the "Ice Bucket Challenge" which rapidly went viral. This campaign, designed to create ALS awareness, resulted in celebrities and others worldwide talking about ALS as they dumped buckets of ice over their heads and nominated others to do so as well.

❖ Corning's "Day Made of Glass" video shared its vision for the future.

❖ To combat negative attitudes toward banks, Deutsch NY introduced the PNC Neighborhood Wishlist on Facebook—which resulted in 500 small grant project submissions and a 550 percent growth in fans.

❖ Duracell aligned with fire departments in a "Those Who Protect Us" online campaign.

❖ OfficeMax educated bloggers on easy ways to get organized and improve home offices.

❖ Maxwell House perked up its corporate image by publicly recommitting to its community service history.

❖ BioDelivery Sciences International, Inc. accepted a variety of online and print interviews to discuss opioid addiction and their related solutions—which got them ready for prime time when Jim Cramer and *Mad Money* came calling for a national airtime segment with the CEO.

❖ Despite increased unemployment, Monster.com reaffirmed its status showcasing new jobseeker technology.

❖ A Morgan Stanley Smith Barney employee said he worked LinkedIn contacts to net $10 million worth of business over 18 months.

❖ Sparky the Firedog's 60th birthday reached a new generation of fans online while educating about fire prevention and safety.

❖ Army Strong opened the military life conversation online with influencers and recruits.

❖ Capital One, the financial services company, engages daily with its 2.5 million Facebook followers.

❖ Band-Aid tapped its inner "fashionista" to brand its adhesive pads as a trendy accessory.

❖ A tax preparation service created a contest on YouTube that earned a record-setting 1.6 million views.

❖ A large accounting firm created a Facebook "friend" community to recruit new graduates just out of college.

❖ Bank of America and HSBC reversed customer-fee decisions after their policies were very publicly attacked online.

❖ A stock brokerage is teaching young adults good financial management habits with its Financial Fitness Quiz available on Twitter.

❖ Princess Cruises cleverly tied into the "bucket list" concept with a "50 Essential Experiences" online campaign.

❖ An investment company is helping people compare their spending, debt and investments with peers via a free web widget.

❖ A credit card company offers its card users a free phone app that helps them find the closest ATMs.

❖ Recognizing the power of online publishing and leading the social conversation, Dian Griesel Int'l. created a new free-for-use news service that showcases corporate brands and management teams. This marketing, branding and advertising site engages current and potential consumers, partners, investors and collaborators.

Hundreds of thousands of people have used the site, which hit a million page views in less than 6 months. Traffic is growing exponentially every day.

Capture the Internet's Power

As we move into Part II, you'll learn proven smart ideas that, if followed, can make it possible for you to harness the power of the Internet, making "friends" for your benefit. Each idea can help you to better market your company, while creating new sales possibilities and partnerships. As you read, keep this in mind: social media is ever-evolving. New, creative ideas for branding companies are being introduced daily. By the time you finish reading this paragraph, it is highly likely that some company will have started to establish a new social networking platform. Diligence, coupled with vigilance in protecting your online presence, will be required. However, be assured the ideas in these pages will likely still apply regardless of what develops, because they are filled with common sense—which hopefully will never be outdated!

CHAPTER 12:

Making Your Website a Fabulous Marketing Brochure

Launching a website without considerable planning is a bad idea. A website can either be a mere placeholder that resides online or a fabulous brochure that takes interaction with your desired audiences to the next level. Planning should begin with careful consideration as to *who* your targeted audiences are, *why* they want to find you, *what* they will be searching for and what you offer to end their search, *when* they need you, *how* you can help them and last but not least, *where* they can find you.

Ideally your site should share just enough information so that visitors are inspired to move to the next level of interaction with your company. When it comes to captivating the attention of those who find your website, quality content—text, images, sound, video or animations, for example—becomes essential. Upon launch, your site will be fresh so people might visit it by chance or simply for its new design, but traffic will die off if people don't have any reason to come back.

A good website informs prospects, leads and customers about your fabulous business. It can also be an opportunity to share quality content that shows your audience that you're an expert in your field and you understand your industry. If carefully conceived and properly designed—with a little extra promotional effort as outlined in these smart ideas—it should reach the first page of results on web search engines.

Let's begin Website Design 101.

SMART IDEA: Find a smart web designer who wants to partner with you to grow your business and stick with you beyond the site's launch day.

If you have ever worked with someone to build your company's website, the process can be terrifying and quickly go up in flames. It can be hard to find a trustworthy and talented designer to catch your vision and represent that well on a website.

But a great website designer/developer will not only create something beautiful, functional, and informational, but they will help you execute your overall communications strategy beyond just your website. They can integrate your email signups, track your website analytics, and provide advice on new trends in the design world to keep you and your business looking fresh and up-to-date.

While some platforms, like Wordpress, are user friendly for smaller sites, there are those sites that are more extensive, networked and complicated. Regardless, having a responsible and reliable webmaster partner on your side is priceless. You will have times when you need to do quick updates, fix bugs, or upload new content-- and an extra hand that can do it almost instinctively is...handy!

I have personally two favorite website designers that I recommend based on the scope of the project. If you'd like to know who they are... give me a call. I can provide the connection and glowing recommendations for their work.

SMART IDEA: Make your site functional, neat, clean and informative.

Before you venture into the social media world, make sure things at home—your website—look good. Give people a user-friendly place to get more information about you, your company, partnership or job opportunities and/or information about purchasing your product or service. You can have the best social media program in place, but if you aren't directing that traffic to an easy-to-navigate site, you're missing huge opportunities.

SMART IDEA: Your website is your modern-day brochure or business card.

The first impression is the lasting impression, so really think about the image you want to project. If you are uncomfortable designing your website on your own, then hire someone to help you. Make sure your site is consistent with your business cards, letterhead, envelopes, brochures and any other marketing materials.

SMART IDEA: Clean and simple sites are best.

Don't overwhelm your visitors. Your website should be attractive and easy to use. It needs to clearly and quickly identify your unique value proposition. Don't make visitors work too hard to get the information they need. If you do, they might give up and visit your competitor instead.

SMART IDEA: Periodically assess your website.

Hopefully, upon its original launch, your site accurately reflected your company. Does it still? Has your company grown? Evolved? Added or changed management? Redefined its corporate philosophy? Is your site still the best it can be? Is it making the best "first impression" for your company?

Find 10 people you trust and ask them to assist you with a qualitative assessment of your website. Request they do so with a critical eye toward user-friendliness and content quality based on your business. Ask if they can share constructive suggestions and advice. You might or might not need to redesign your website but you *do* need to know what others think of it. You also need to conduct periodic reviews if your business, products, services or management changes in any way.

SMART IDEA: Continually analyze your website.

Not only do you need to know if your website is working—you also need to know if it's working *optimally*. The best quantitative way to accomplish this is by using web analytics. There are many programs that will track the stats on your website. Google Analytics or Yahoo Web Analytics are great starts. These programs will tell you how many visitors you've had, how long they stayed, where they are from, their ages and more. After you analyze the data you can decide if you need to make improvements, or be rewarded with the concrete knowledge that your site is performing as it should.

Other quantitative analytic measurements can be found by using sites such as Alexa and Compete. These allow you to track a website's rank among all others. You can also compare your website traffic and your competitors'.

SMART IDEA: Learn about search engine optimization (SEO).

There are many ways to master ever-evolving and sometimes mysterious search engine optimization. Many claim to be experts who know the secrets—but beware. There are no tricks that Google and other search engines aren't uncovering every day. Don't waste your hard-earned money on gimmicks. Instead, when carefully planning the design or redesign of your website, consider the likely words that people might contextually search when trying to find your company. Do a Google search without using your company's name, but instead using words that relate to what your company sells, develops, creates, invents, solves or whatever. If your site shows up anywhere in the first one to five pages, your site or PR program is likely working on your behalf. If not, keep reading and learn how you can improve your search results.

Content, links, language, keywords, photo selection and video are all essential and important factors that can help draw traffic to your site, which hopefully means better business for you. The general rule of thumb is that the more organically you can boost your rank, the more staying power that higher rank will have. In this case, organic means simply that your content is relevant, so people seek it regularly.

SMART IDEA: The more links to other websites you have, the more "trusted" you are in the SEO world and the more likely you are to advance closer to page one when searched.

Links are connections between your site and others. Placements in online media outlets that link back to your site within a story are among the most powerful ways to enhance people's ability to find your company online. The more trusted the site is, the better it is for you. For example, a story about your company on FOX News online, CNN online or ABC online that provides a link to your site gives your company greater SEO credibility, which in turn usually equals more favorable positioning in searches. The more of these media placements featuring your company, the better it is for you because it will help people organically find you.

SMART IDEA: Diligently work to improve your "bounce rate."

You not only need people to *find* your website; you also need to *keep* them there. The longer they stay, the greater your odds of a sale, new investor or new partner.

When people land on your site, the quantitative analytic software I mentioned in an earlier rule can determine how long they stay. The length of the visit is calculated in a couple of ways, namely page views and length of stay or bounce rate. Your bounce rate will tell you what percentage of people found your site—but left it rapidly because the content didn't match their expectations. You want a bounce rate of 50 percent or lower. On the other hand, page view analytics will tell you how much time the visitor spent scoping out your content.

These numbers are important. Any good advertising or public relations campaign will focus on driving traffic to your site. The content has to keep visitors interested in learning more. If your bounce rate is high, you might need to tweak your content or site map so you're not wasting opportunities.

A great way to reduce your bounce rate is to have a short video of less than two minutes on your home page—just don't make it open without permission, which tends to aggravate people and make them leave quickly.

People tend to like videos. See if you can make one that helps visitors understand your value proposition, induces them to stay awhile and encourages visits to other pages on your site to learn more.

SMART IDEA: Know thy competitor.

Stay up-to-date on what your competitors are doing. Visit their websites with a mindset geared toward your own improvement, not to steal from them. Knowing your competitors can be as simple as googling them, subscribing to their newsletters, visiting their websites, tracking their news releases, reading their analyst reports and purchasing competitive intelligence software that tracks how their website rank is doing versus yours. The goal is to know how your competitors are performing so you can get an idea of the direction they are going in.

Tracking your competitors' data can help you analyze new market opportunities, assess potential competitive challenges and help you gain an overall better understanding of your positioning within a sector.

SMART IDEA: Optimize your website for desktop and mobile devices.

More and more people are browsing the web via mobile devices. Analysts estimate that by the end of 2015, mobile devices will become the primary means by which most users will access online content.

To stay competitive, you need to have versions of your website optimized for desktop and mobile. They must be glitch-free and must run on iPads, iPhones, Android or any other mobile platform that comes along. Your mobile site can be different than your desktop site. Ideally, a mobile site should be more streamlined, optimized for smaller screens—easy to read, larger buttons—and must require less data to load and run. For business, it's no longer just about the desktop world; mobile is equally important.

CHAPTER 13:

Email Is *Free* Mail

Email is very powerful. That power can work for you—or against you. Its positive or negative impact is far greater than most other highly touted social media platforms on the Internet. According to a report by ecommerce software firm Monetate, only about 0.59 percent of people who come to visit a sales landing page or website via social media actually buy anything. Those who visit sites via Twitter also tend to spend less than visitors who find sites via other marketing strategies. Are you surprised, considering all the hype regarding how we need more social media strategies? Don't be. Searches on search engines such as Google are estimated to raise the conversion rate of visitors to sales to 2.49 percent. But the biggest ally in your free Internet arsenal? Statistics show that a well-written email delivers a return averaging 4.25 percent.

So what does this mean to you?

❖ Social media is best used to engage with consumers who are getting to know a brand. It is the exploratory medium that does not necessarily translate into a transaction. Think of it as a free way to establish your brand.

❖ Search is the first signal of an intention to buy. It is used for "re"-search about a brand and is also a first connection to a brand's site or other information floating around the web. Search engines corroborate credibility—especially if your company is naturally found on the first pages.

❖ Email is for building trust with potential customers who have willingly opted in to learn more via your communications. Ultimately, it is your way of sharing your intention to sell something—whether a service, idea, partnership or otherwise. Think of it as your social media tool to help facilitate the "close."

What makes email such a dynamic method of marketing is that the messages sent can be targeted far more effectively. Specific messages can be sent to each segment of your audience, not just demographic segments but behavioral segments as well. Most importantly, if used right, email begins direct negotiation. This is something Twitter is unlikely to deliver, and tweets are appealing to only a fraction of the receiving audience, making Twitter the polar opposite of targeted marketing.

As with anything in life, there are right ways to utilize email, this free and fabulous form of communication, as well as wrong and annoying ways to use it.

The smart ideas in this chapter will cover the creative ways in which you can amp your ability to get your emails opened, read and actionable. It will also share common errors guaranteed to keep your emails unopened and your email address tagged to go directly to the spam file of your intended recipient.

Let's begin!

SMART IDEA: Reporters like to be properly pitched by email.

Here's an email lesson overview. Then, throughout this chapter, I'll delve into several of these points further so you can fully understand the value of these smart ideas!

Done correctly, reporters like email because:

❖ Emails are typically short, keeping "fluff" to a minimum.

❖ The email is easy to delete if they're not interested—a double-edged sword.

❖ They can review your pitch at their leisure.

❖ They can easily respond with questions seeking more information to gauge the possibilities of your suggested story angles and content.

Success comes if you customize your email lists and personalize the email. Remember—if you blast random emails, you might suffer the consequences of getting banned permanently by reporters!

Use your subject line creatively and effectively. Then, do spam checks of that subject line to avoid getting filtered and trashed before arriving at your ultimate destination. Don't forget: a killer headline is still essential.

To capture attention, get personal with your subject line:

❖ Try placing *News, Press Info* or *Story Idea* at the beginning of your subject line in brackets.

❖ Incorporate the reporter's first name at the beginning of the subject line.

❖ If the targeted reporter has a regular column, use the title of their column in the subject line.

❖ If the reporter doesn't write a regular column, but is known to cover a particular topic in his or her beat, highlight it. For example: "Bill—story idea for the plastics industry."

❖ Avoid words like sex, new, exclusive, revolutionary, powerful and the like, which sound tacky and tend to be caught by spam filters in any case.

❖ Never send an email with a blank subject line.

Email body basics:

❖ Highlight your news as clearly as possible.

❖ Avoid multiple or, for that matter, *any* exclamation points.

❖ Customize the story to the reporter's needs.

❖ Use uppercase and lowercase letters, which are easier to read than all caps.

❖ Don't try to be too cute or too vague. Get to the point in the first line or two.

❖ Don't make the reporter scroll to the story. Respect reporters' time or you will lose them.

❖ Make mention of any recent story by that reporter relevant to your field of interest. Provide positive comments about the story and tell them if they write about the topic again, they should get in touch with you because you can provide expert opinion, additional facts or support.

❖ Include your phone number. This adds credibility and allows a reporter the opportunity to pick up the phone and call you to discuss an idea they find intriguing.

❖ Spell-check and reread your email before you send it. Email deserves the same proper grammar, punctuation and spelling as a letter to the President of the United States.

❖ Do not include attachments. With all the viruses prevalent today, most reporters automatically delete emails with attachments from unknown senders. Wait for the reporter to request additional attached information.

An email campaign alone does not constitute an effective public relations plan. However, it is a solid and important aspect of your overall program.

SMART IDEA: Include an email address, website and (perhaps) an offer on your business card.

Most business people use their business card as a basic tool designed to deliver their contact information. At the very least, this should include your name, address and phone number, along with your email and possibly your full corporate website.

Every time you pass your card to someone, your goal should be to get them to send you an email so you can begin building your opted-in, full permission granted, email list.

Savvy businesspeople add an offer on the back of their cards to provoke a response. Include some kind of offer to get the recipient to begin a dialog for future marketing purposes. Think about what you can offer. A newsletter, industry updates and instant updates on your developments are all possibilities. Use your imagination. Make your card a sales tool by adding a special email address designed to collect email addresses for use in your future marketing campaigns.

SMART IDEA: Master the art of making third-party email introductions.

If I were to sum up what I do for work, I'd say I make very qualified introductions.

I'm a "connector," according to Malcolm Gladwell. I've been creating introductions for people throughout my entire life. I'm well-paid monetarily, socially and emotionally for connecting people with other people who are likely to benefit from my introductions—*if* they take the initiative and follow up.

The introductions I make are beneficial not only to those I'm connecting, but also to me. Each is a customized extension of my personal brand. They allow me to show others the wide scope of influential people that I know well enough to help open doors. This power is immense because it showcases my personal and professional reach, and is an easy way to be generous. Generosity is ultimate power.

Although I make plenty of in-person introductions at events, along with enlisting the telephone, today the large majority of the relationships I create for others start with an email.

The format for these emails is easy to follow and intentionally so.

First off, I get to the point by clearly stating in the subject line: An Introduction for Business.

My opening paragraph reiterates that I'm making an introduction. I then give a little context as to how I know each person and what their talents are. I then elaborate on why I think these people should get connected—even if I only say "I'm not exactly sure what business I think you can do together, but I do think an exploratory conversation is worth your time."

Then I tell them I've made the intro and the rest is up to them. It is now their jobs to determine whether they want to explore the relationship.

SMART IDEA: Be gracious and responsive to those who make email introductions for you.

If someone has taken the time to create an email introduction on your behalf, be gracious and responsive.

In your first response, which should be sent within 24 hours, be sure to copy the introducer and begin with a "thank you" to that person for their generosity.

Then be direct and propose your suggestion for the next step of a follow-up phone call or meeting. Don't send a long email about yourself or your business at this point. Direct person-to-person contact is what is warranted now to begin exploring this possible new relationship. I read very little about anything prior to a personal phone call.

Once a call or meeting is established, make sure to allot equal time towards finding out not just how the person might help you, but how you can be beneficial to them as well.

After you've connected, be sure to drop a quick email to the original introducer and share a little color regarding how the first meeting or call went. They'll be curious to know if they made a "match" and it is another chance for you to be gracious.

SMART IDEA: Follow the Batman comic book strategy.

Did you ever read a good old comic book? I'm talking about the ones where the action was defined by capital POW! BANG! BOOM!

Make sure your subject has POW! Short subject lines relaying value are better. Typical inboxes only show 60 characters; mobile phones 25 to 30. This means five to eight words max (logical business abbreviations are okay).

Your opening line is BANG! It consists of the most important words at the beginning of the first paragraph.

Your closing line has BOOM! It creates urgency by setting a time-frame if you need a response.

POW! BANG! BOOM! is the formula that results in ACTION!

SMART IDEA: Use logical words in your subject lines.

Every one of us has spent time searching for an email we want to recall for one reason or another. The search is always easier when the sender used a word in the subject line that logically relates to the content of the email.

This same principle applies to emails you might send to someone in the media. A reporter or producer might read an email and decide to save it for a future story. On the day they are finally ready to pull up notes about your company, the odds of seeing coverage improve greatly if you have helped them by following this rule and making your email easy to find. Always use words that logically relate to your story idea in the subject line.

SMART IDEA: If it's timely news, put a deadline in the subject line.

If you are announcing news or offering a timely interview opportunity—versus a story that will be "evergreen"—put a deadline in your subject line for greater response.

Use phrases such as: Please reply by; Timely information; Deadline. Do not use this strategy for every angle you pitch or you will be dumped in the trash and disbelieved like "the boy who cried wolf." But do use this smart idea if the interview opportunity is truly timely, as every reporter will appreciate receiving fair notice and a deadline within which action is required.

SMART IDEA: Do not start a sentence in the subject line...

...and finish it in the email. This *faux pas* is probably at the top of my "immediately delete" list. It is beyond annoying—a ploy I perceive as a trick to try to get me to open an email that is likely to be a waste of my time. Don't try to force or trick a reporter into opening an email. They might fall for it once. But then they might delete your annoying emails and possibly add your name to their spam filter.

SMART IDEA: Always be asking for email addresses and request permission to send email to those who supply them.

One-on-one meetings, group lunches or dinners, trade shows and conferences are all opportunities to collect business cards and email addresses.

When presenting at a conference, be bold. Get a small business card holder—the kind with the plastic pages that have little compartments to hold business cards. When you start your presentation, show everyone your business card holder. Tell them you will be passing it around during your presentation and you would love to have them insert their business card into one of the slots, and then pass it to the person next to them to do the same. At the end of your presentation, you might have a valuable book that includes the full contact information of a group of people who are interested in being kept up-to-date about your developments.

At trade shows, use a fishbowl next to a bowl filled with candy or some other fun, inexpensive premium. Most people are happy to exchange their card for some form of freebie.

Bottom line: if you don't ask, you won't get. Ask for those business cards and be sure to have a consistent system to import all the email addresses for future marketing purposes.

SMART IDEA: "Content" isn't just about being online.

Putting content online is a great business branding and building strategy. But one of my issues with social media is that many have thrown the baby out with the bathwater to jump on the Internet bandwagon. This is a mistake.

Today, smart public relations managers acknowledge that the Internet is becoming a crowded marketplace, simply because it is largely a free way to get your message out. However, spending a few dollars to send a *paper* newsletter to existing customers might be a good strategy to build loyalty and better repeat business.

Customer newsletters don't have to be fancy in format or printing. In fact, surveys show they work better when they don't get too fancy. Four-color printing on glossy paper looks like an ad. A simple photocopy on plain paper looks like valuable inside information.

Think of your mailing as a letter you'd send a friend. Give them an update about all the wonderful things going on in your life—and close by suggesting you get together or requiring some other action by the recipient.

Remember, when the pool is getting crowded, there are still plenty of other places to swim. So along with collecting emails—try to collect traditional address as well.

ENGAGE: Smart Ideas to Get More Media Coverage,
Build Your Influence and Grow Your Business

SMART IDEA: Include a sign-up link in your emails.

If you are trying to build an email list—and you are!—you must ask and ask again for permission to send emails to everyone you know. Adding a sign-up link, embedded right into your emails, is an easy way to troll for those coveted email addresses. A simple line stating: "Click here to receive our newsletter highlighting corporate developments and news" is very effective.

SMART IDEA: Work your address book.

MailChimp.com is amazing and a must have for online marketing. MailChimp offers easy-to-use, inexpensive options for keeping your mailing list, or many separate lists, on standby and ready to work for you at all times.

To get an email list ready, export your address book and upload it to a service like MailChimp. MailChimp will automatically check for duplicates. Prepare a friendly and very brief email asking those in your address book if they would like to opt-in to receive all your future emails as well. Getting permission must always be your priority. Then keep your contacts up-to-date with relevant, interesting news and offers.

Note: MailChimp has a "white list" policy. No purchased lists are permitted to be uploaded; only names that you've collected personally and been given permission to use can be imported.

SMART IDEA: Use an online RSVP when you host your next event.

If you are planning an event, consider doing the registration for it electronically. Insist that all attendees sign up via your website and that they leave an email address for confirmation.

Be sure to state that email addresses will not be sold—and respect your own policy—but that they might be used for further updates and news.

SMART IDEA: Send "happy birthday" emails.

On my birthday, I was surprised to receive a "happy birthday" email from the dealership where I had recently purchased a car.

The email offered birthday wishes. No promotion was included. Yet I could see the dealership had established a cross-referenced database of customers, which most likely triggered an automatic birthday wishes email.

This little gesture not only made me smile, it also subtly reminded me it was time to book an oil change. As the purchase was a pleasant experience, it reinforced that I liked this particular dealership and reminded me to refer them to others.

Could sending birthday wishes keep you in the forefront of the minds of potential customers, partners, investors or the media? You betcha!

SMART IDEA: Make email address collection a corporate game.

Successful companies harness all their employees' help when there is a mission to accomplish. If you want to build an email list, incentivize your employees to gain their enthusiasm for this project.

Set a deadline and a goal. Give each business card a value appropriate to your overall business plan. Encourage each employee to strive to win whatever reward you have established for obtaining the greatest number of email addresses. As you gather the addresses, be sure to send an email requesting permission to mail future news and developments. Be sure to award the prize. Consider making this a monthly contest for your employees, and make sure you assign someone the job of loading the contact information into the appropriate email list for future marketing outreach.

SMART IDEA: Ask for a referral.

If a client is happy, they are usually open to the idea of providing a referral. In your email signature block, consider adding a line that says, "If you are happy with our service, perhaps you'd like to make an email introduction to a friend or associate. We value your opinion and recommendation highly."

Again, with email, it's all about asking to get!

SMART IDEA: Send emails even when you don't need something.

This is not an invitation to waste anyone else's time.

Instead, consider a policy of sending out one or two daily emails with something very specific to a person(s) with whom you want to network. Find an article relevant to their interests. If they've recently been in the media, send the clip and say "Saw this and you sounded/looked great!" or "it made me think of you." Make it about the other person, focused on what they need—and you'll likely make a friend.

SMART IDEA: Convert your mailing list to an email list.

If you have a postal list without emails, consider designing a direct mail offer that can be spelled out on a postcard.

Offer the "prize" only to those who submit their email address.

One of our clients had over a million Facebook "likes." They wanted to convert those Facebook followers into a corporate email list. To accomplish this goal, they hosted a Facebook campaign: they directed their "friends" to enter a contest that simply required entering their email address and other contact information on the corporate website. In return, each received a chance to win two tickets to a star-studded event in California that the company was hosting. The company succeeded in converting a couple hundred of those fans per day into a marketable corporate email list.

SMART IDEA: Never send an email saying something you wouldn't say in person to the recipient, or an email that would embarrass you if blasted across the Internet and newspapers worldwide.

When you are **H**ungry, **A**ngry, **L**onely or **T**ired: **HALT**. Don't sit down at your computer and write anything until you can express yourself unemotionally and with clear, methodical thinking. You won't feel better for having whipped off a nasty email. Instead, you will feel like a jerk—assuming you have an ounce of moral fiber in your body.

Feeling anxious, angry, frustrated, confused or any other emotion based on insecurity or fear? Get up, take a walk, breathe deeply and calm yourself down. Then, when you are calm, reread the email you are about to send and rewrite it if necessary or delete it.

If, on the other hand, you *receive* a nasty email, ask these three questions:

1. Does this contain valuable information I need to perform better?
2. Is this simply criticism and/or frustration from the sender?
3. Is this simply worth deleting because it has no value?

If it is number one, do whatever you have to do to improve what requires improvement. If it is number two, call the sender and calmly and directly ask, "What's up with that email?" If it is number three, delete it and get on with your fabulous life!

SMART IDEA: Beware of weekend and late evening emails.

Email and social media have blurred the lines of respect in a variety of ways. One of them is mailing and sharing things that are not necessarily appropriate or welcomed by the recipient. Always be aware that the person reading that email has their own set of feelings and morals... and a life! Just because you've written a message doesn't mean it must be sent the moment it was penned—or ever! This is what your "Drafts" folder is for.

Learn to use your "Drafts" folder on weekends and late evenings when you have the urge to send an email that could wait until Monday or the next day.

Everyone needs downtime in this high-tech, technology-tied-to-the-hip age. Respect the free time and lives of others. And on that note, define boundaries and show that you respect your own free time—and have a life outside of work—as well.

SMART IDEA: Make sure CAPS are OFF!

Capitalization in email is the equivalent of YELLING! DO YOU WANT TO GET YELLED AT? I don't. Neither do others.

SMART IDEA: Include opt-in forms on every page on your website.

Every page of your website should have an easy-to-find link for your visitors to opt-in for receiving future news and offers.

Consider adding pop-up windows to your site to make this more impactful.

Design your site so that when someone attempts to leave it, a window pops up and asks if they *really* want to leave—and if they'd like to provide their email address to receive future updates.

SMART IDEA: Include a forward-to-a-friend link in your emails and on your website.

On DGIwire.com, my copyright-free-content website, new articles are written and posted daily that are free for publishers, producers, bloggers, reporters and others to reprint for publication and/or airing. The site makes it very easy to print the article and it is also very easy to email it to yourself or someone else as well.

If you have a blog on your website or information that visitors might like to share with others, you can design your site in such a way that in order to print the information, a name and email address is required.

There is one company's site I visit often for health information. The company not only sends me daily emails with some kind of news update, but the emails are live links to the site where the news is hosted. When I visit, if I like what I see and want to send it to myself or someone else, I enter my intended recipients' names and email addresses, along with the note I want to send, and off goes my email. So this clever company has me building their mailing list because I'm compelled to share their information with my friends and associates. So far, no one has complained!

So be sure to include a forward-to-a-friend link on every page of your site.

SMART IDEA: Offer "email list only" discounts.

If you can apply this rule to your business, it's a very valuable way to get your clients, customers, associates and friends to start working for you.

Here's how it works: if you can occasionally offer an exclusive discount to those on your email list, do it. But be sure to include a line to the effect of: "If you know someone who might also like to receive these special discounts, please send us their email address."

Don't use these offers anywhere else: reserve them exclusively for those who have generously given you the opportunity to email them.

JetBlue does a fine job utilizing this special email list tactic. I get email-list-only offers for great flight discounts. If you want to get on their special list—of which I am a proud member—let me know! They've made me an enthusiastic, unpaid promoter.

SMART IDEA: Ask for what you want.

How many emails have you received and wondered, "What the heck does this person want?"

Too many business emails are written as if the sender were having a casual phone conversation. Write less and say more with carefully chosen words. Get to the point. Define the call to action. Get to "the ask."

Don't make the recipient wonder "what's the point?" or you've wasted your precious time and theirs.

SMART IDEA: Remember email when telemarketing. No hang-ups allowed until you ask for an email address.

If you use telemarketing to promote your business, you have a golden opportunity. Don't ever hang up on a business call without asking for the other party's email address. You can say you'd like to have it so you can stay in touch or because you want to send them updates. Again—if you don't ask, you won't get. But if you *do* ask, you might find that with each call you make, you are accruing a great email list that can be used as a follow-up sales tactic.

Now that we've addressed email, let's take a closer look at friends and followers.

CHAPTER 14:

The Power of Social Media

Is social media becoming unsociable?

For many, social media outlets such as Facebook, Twitter and Google+, started out as fun and easy ways for people to connect. Yet today, according to a recent survey done by E-Score, it has become a time-consuming chore—and the results for time invested are highly questionable. According to the survey, although awareness and usage of social media are extremely high, the allure of using these sites is starting to wear thin. The survey further revealed that when considering a purchase, consumers trust traditional media—national newspapers, magazines, trade publications, television, cable, radio and their online outlets—exponentially more than social media.

According to the survey, both Facebook and Twitter—with approximately 140 million and 92 million monthly visitors, respectively—have surprisingly low appeal ratings, suggesting the sites are more habit-forming than a resource. Providing more information about the trend toward unsociability is the fact that Yelp—which has a low level of overall awareness—had the highest appeal and greatest number of users, indicating a preference for social media sites providing on-demand, relevant information versus merely interaction with others. Strong websites can also accomplish this goal.

Persistent reports of the death of traditional media are often wildly exaggerated. Still, there is no doubt that the media and marketing landscape has changed significantly, as all of us can now go to our favorite sites to find articles and information of interest, often at no cost. Community news is no longer confined to cul-de-sacs: it's online and far-reaching. We can find out what people are saying about an issue, a product or a company on sites like Twitter, Facebook, Google+, Pinterest, Instagram and countless more; by reading our favorite blogs; or by watching up-to-the-minute videos on YouTube. Still, none of this means that the major daily newspapers, weekly newsmagazines, and highly regarded national and local TV and radio talk shows—especially those centered on business, news and investment—have lost their allure.

Odds favor that you would like your company to be featured in national, regional or trade print; on radio; and on TV or cable. Even if audiences have shifted somewhat, these remain prestigious media outlets. Whenever you are on the business media circuit, you are reaching specific targeted audiences; the size of the audience—quantity—is secondary to quality.

Today, all companies can benefit from using social media to reach out to their current and potential investors, and *all* forms of media for the timely dissemination of information and to attract new interest. Why should a company care about social media? Because we now live in a globally connected world, one in which investors and customers can gather critical information about your company in minutes instead of weeks or months.

Caveat: SEC Compliance Regulations Apply for Public Companies

With all the excitement and fun of social media, don't think there aren't any rules! Public companies developing a social media presence must consider compliance with Securities and Exchange Commission (SEC) regulations. In particular, Regulation FD (Fair Disclosure) prohibits the selective disclosure of material information. Potential pitfalls of using social media include violations of Regulation FD, as well as disclosure of confidential information, and possible actions for invasion of privacy or defamation.

The SEC has issued reports that outline the boundaries for sharing information. It has also put companies on notice that they and their employees will be held liable for the information they post on blogs, networks, online communities and discussion forums. Although the SEC continues to update and refine these guidelines, no public company should adopt a wait-and-see attitude toward the dangers inherent in employee use of social media. Indeed, one wrong, irresponsible post on Facebook or casual comment on Twitter can result in unprecedented consequences that trigger SEC and/or shareholder or customer retaliation.

Prior to social media, if a customer had a complaint about your product or company or service, the word might have been limited to family members along with some friends. Today, this dissatisfaction can go viral in moments. Papa John's, a pizzeria chain, experienced this the hard way. In early 2012, one of their employees printed a racial slur on a customer receipt at one of the chain's New York City outlets. The customer promptly retaliated by tweeting and posting a photo of the receipt on the Internet. Management at Papa John's responded quickly with a public apology and fired the employee. Interestingly, in the wake of the event as people stood on the sidelines waiting to observe the company's response, Papa John's' swift crisis management actions gained it new fans since action was quick and apologetic.

The obvious problem is the overlapping of personal and corporate use of social media. It's not enough to caution company representatives to use common sense in such matters. Although the use of social media by public corporations is in their interest, and they would be foolish not to engage these platforms, social media on the personal level has been around long enough that many people will assume they know how to use it and might dangerously disregard the compliance regulations established for more traditional media.

By way of example, a public relations firm lost an automotive giant as a client when one of the employees of that PR firm happened to be sitting in a traffic jam and mindlessly tweeted something to the effect of: "I don't know why Detroit is called the Motor City. You can't @#^&ing get anywhere!" The automobile giant didn't take kindly to the slur against its hometown and promptly fired the firm, taking its highly lucrative account to a competitor communications firm—likely one that was drilled about its employee social media policies!

The existing SEC guidance about dissemination of corporate news on the Internet primarily addresses when information posted on a company website is "public" for purposes of Regulation FD, and company liability for information on websites. The SEC has recognized that companies may post information, and have that information be considered "disseminated," without having to place the same information on a newswire or on a Form 8-K. But unless you are the CEO of a large cap company, following this could be highly dangerous and problematic.

As most companies are now aware, Regulation FD prohibits selective disclosure of material nonpublic information. The main two principles are 1) that companies are required to publicly disclose any material information that they disclose selectively, and 2) selective disclosure of material information that is already public will not violate the regulation. When the SEC first adopted Regulation FD in 2000, it acknowledged that companies might be able to rely solely on the web to disseminate disclosure at some point in the future. However, it emphasized that web disclosure alone was not likely to be considered sufficient.

The guidance further states, "Since all communications made by, or on behalf of, a company are subject to the antifraud provisions of the federal securities laws, companies should consider taking steps to put into place controls and procedures to monitor statements made by or on behalf of the company on these types of electronic forums."

Corporate policy regarding social media should also outline what should not be discussed or addressed on employee blogs, tweets or Facebook pages, etc., and should incorporate applicable federal securities law obligations governing the dissemination of information for public companies. Where necessary, they might also require the use of standard disclaimers.

Interestingly, the SEC itself has its own Twitter account, and encourages companies to communicate to investors via the web. In July 2009, the Commission said companies could disseminate certain information on the web without issuing a news release. Still, some companies remain hesitant to jump in. A vice president of investor relations for Intel was once quoted as saying, "There's always going to be a person with an axe to grind. Do we really want to sponsor that?" Intel was among the first companies to allow shareholders to ask questions via the web and vote online during its annual meeting. However, the company avoided blogs and Twitter for investor issues, because it feared violating SEC disclosure rules or inviting public criticism in a company-hosted forum.

Kenneth Cole Productions, Inc., a company that has been aggressive in many of its advertising campaigns and use of social media, might have liked to have been a bit more informed about social media quips before it experienced a misuse of social media that created a reputational threat.

The Kenneth Cole campaigns are often aligned with current news events. Attempting to promote their 2011 collection, the company sent out a tweet that quipped about an uprising in Cairo—a historical event in itself as it had been organized by a social media campaign. Many thousands of people went to Twitter and Facebook to voice their outrage and disapproval. Kenneth Cole was derailed and forced to apologize, engage and issue tweets of regrets. The flipside is that they acted and managed the event effectively, and in doing so gained thousands of new followers. Certainly it is not the best business practice to attempt to raise your brand via bad publicity—but heck, when in hot water you better know how to swim and get out of it quickly without getting burned.

All companies should devise a social media policy before adopting blogs, Facebook, Twitter or whatever outlet becomes hot next. It would also be wise for any company to include the standard disclaimers used in other communications; and these "social" communications certainly shouldn't disclose financial or other information that isn't available elsewhere! In addition, any Internet site should clearly state that opinions expressed by others in company-sponsored forums—like comments on blogs—do not represent management's views. Many a CEO has seen their valuation take a big hit, one they sometimes never recover from—especially if they don't have a crisis management strategy in place—after a follower took offense at a posted comment and angrily responded.

No matter how misinformed and unfair commentary might be about you or your company, responding in kind is usually the wrong strategy. Don't jump into the fray at all. Put out positive news and keep on putting it out—but do it on your website, in a news release, on a respected wire service, in the blogosphere and in all media. Make sure whatever material you put out deals with and corrects incorrect or attacking comments and misconceptions, but without specifically citing the exact negative comments. You don't want to use your PR machine to give naysayers any unnecessary attention or make their comments more searchable!

Fight fire (negative comments) with your own brand of fire (your positive news coverage) and in so doing, put the fire out! Of primary importance here, however, is ensuring that your company has a current and relevant corporate media strategy in place. This strategy must clearly articulate your company's position regarding employee participation on social media sites, including your corporate site(s), as well as what your employees are allowed to say about your company and your company's products on their private sites.

Traditional versus Social Media

Let's review and make sure you understand what social media is, and how it can be put to work for you by your team.

Traditional media include television, cable, radio, newspapers and film. The term social media, which some businesses also call "consumer-generated media (CGM)," means using web-based and mobile technologies to create interactive dialogue. A common thread running through all definitions of social media is a blending of technology and social interaction for the co-creation of value. In this context, value means the benefit to all parties involved in a communication, be it education, enlightenment, entertainment, enjoyment, connection, recognition or whatever else is gained by the interaction. Social media is, of course, digital—it exists on computers and handheld devices. Today's leading social media outlets include Facebook, Twitter, YouTube, LinkedIn and Google+, with sites like Instagram and Pinterest rising very rapidly up the usage ranks. More are on the horizon. The majority of these and other outlets are free and readily accessible. They allow private individuals as well as companies to publish or access information.

Acknowledging the differences between the two groups of mass communication—traditional versus social—the question becomes, what is the most effective way to distribute information via social media? And how much weight should still be placed on traditional media?

One characteristic shared by social and traditional media is the ability to reach small or large audiences; for example, both a YouTube video and a national newspaper can reach just a small number of people or an audience of millions. Traditional media, however, typically use a centralized framework for organization, production and dissemination, whereas social media are, by their very nature, more decentralized, less hierarchical and distinguished by multiple points of production and dissemination.

In business, measurements of success include reputation and revenues. In social media, it is share of voice, how your material resonates and the support and response it receives. Engagement data include measurement of clicks, fans, friends, followers, views and check-ins. Although it is not an exact science and there is a good deal of debate surrounding the value of these kinds of metrics in the different business sectors, it is important to understand each and how they are derived so that you can judge their individual worth for yourself. After all, even Facebook, the company that created the virtual friend phenomenon, is now downplaying the importance of your number of "friends." Of far more importance is how a particular post might resonate and inspire subsequent "sharing" with friends and followers.

Marketing Yourself as a "Social Authority"

Social authority is developed when an individual or organization establishes him, her or themselves as an "expert" in their given business or professional arena. It is through this process of building social authority and becoming an influencer in that arena that social media becomes an effective tool. Although you can never completely control your message through social media, you can begin to participate in the ongoing communication or "conversation" in hopes of becoming a relevant influencer in that communication. This conversation participation requires subtle and clever execution. People are resistant to marketing in general, but even more resistant to direct or overt marketing through social media. A marketer can generally not expect people to be receptive to a marketing message in and of itself. In fact, many sites/blogs will not let you participate if you are overtly trying to sell a product or market your wares.

Effective marketing today can benefit from carefully crafted "messages" posted on social media by *trusted sources*. The use of social media as a form of marketing is another tool in an overall plan. Marketing efforts by business adding this tool to their communications strategies must strive to convince people of their genuine intentions, knowledge and expertise in their specific area or industry. This is not really a "new" concept: The new aspect is that "low key" and indirect messages seem to resonate. The best efforts involve providing valuable and accurate information on an ongoing basis without an obvious associated marketing angle. If trust in the source is there, the message itself begins to develop naturally. This person and his or her organization then becomes a trusted "advisor" instead of a marketer. The benefit here is that the consumer begins to naturally gravitate to the products and/or offerings of the authority/influencer.

There are many ways to use social media to create authority and influence. The well-known platforms include Wikipedia, Facebook, Twitter, Instagram, Pinterest and Reddit; posting articles and blogs on e-zines; and Scribd, for starters. One can also provide fact-based answers on "social question-and-answer sites" such as EHow and Yahoo! Answers and others.

There is no doubt that some of today's consumers are likely to consider buying decisions based on what they read and see on social media platforms. Studies reveal that organizations have also been able, through social media channels, to bring back dissatisfied customers and stakeholders. This is why a purposeful and carefully designed social media strategy has become essential to any marketing plan—and the first step is to become adept at these newer "authority building" techniques.

By example, Zappos, the online shoe retailer, has successfully harnessed social media to build its corporate identity and culture. Zappos CEO Tony Hsieh came up with the idea of a company-wide Twitter stream so that his employees could share insight and feedback they were likely to get during their off hours. The stream eventually expanded to include customers, creating a virtually free source of market testing and feedback, which attracted customers to Zappos' relational culture. Hsieh himself regularly posts on Twitter and has developed a loyal following. These innovative strategies have helped build Zappos into the leading online shoe store.

Let's take a look at a few of the current leading social media sites available for your use today.

LinkedIn

LinkedIn defines itself as a social networking website designed for business professionals. It allows you to share work-related information with other users and keep an online list of professional contacts. You are allowed to create a custom profile. However, profiles created within LinkedIn are business-oriented rather than personal. For example, a LinkedIn profile highlights education and past work experience, which makes it appear similar to a resume. Profiles also list your connections to other LinkedIn users, as well as recommendations you make or receive from other users.

By using LinkedIn, you can keep in touch with past and current colleagues, which can be useful in today's ever-changing work environment. You can also connect with new people when looking for potential business partners. Although people outside your personal network cannot view your full profile, they can still view a snapshot of your education and work experience. Others can also contact you using LinkedIn's anonymous "InMail" messaging service, which could lead to new job opportunities or business relationships.

LinkedIn has several benefits for business professionals, which is why it is used by millions of people across the world. Just remember, if you decide to create a LinkedIn profile, keep your information professional. It's best to save your personal information for the other social networking websites.

Also important to note: A great business networking strategy is to not accept someone into your LinkedIn network unless you know him or her or have spoken with him or her. I suggest you try this. As mentioned above, your LinkedIn network can be likened to an online Rolodex. Personally, I'm not concerned about building a large fanbase on LinkedIn. Rather, I want to make sure that if I'm linked to someone, I can speak highly of them and freely offer them recommendations, connections or referrals. When someone asks to join my network whom I don't know, I review their LinkedIn profile and either delete the request or send a note saying I'd be happy to have a conversation before accepting—as I don't usually connect to people I don't know. This has led to some really interesting calls. However, I currently have more than 600 people on my "wait to have a call" list. Networking is a time-consuming process if you want to do it effectively.

Google+

Google+ (pronounced Google plus) is a Google social networking project. The Google+ design team sought to replicate the way people interact offline more closely than is the case with other social networking services such as Facebook and Twitter.

Google+ promotes "circles" that enable you to categorize your connections, so you can share updates selectively with different groups. Examples of such groups might include family, friends, office colleagues and people you share particular interests with. Circles might be discrete or overlap, so that, for example, someone you work with who's also in your book club will get updates for both groups. Users outside a circle can see a list of member names but not the name of the circle.

Hangouts are an option for video chat for up to 10 people at any given time. Google's emphasis is on creating the kind of space that replicates casual ad-hoc gatherings in the real world.

Huddle is an option for text message group chats, for Android, iPhone and SMS devices.

Instant upload is an option to automatically send pictures and videos taken with a cell phone to a private photo album. Users can then decide whether to share them and which circles to share them with.

Streams are similar to Facebook news updates but you can see updates for particular circles rather than updates for everyone at once.

Sparks are topics that you want to discuss with others. The interface is an adaptation of Google search. Google describes it this way: "The friends you have are the ones who allow you to geek out about what you are absolutely passionate about…and they have enough of a commonality to let you explore it."

Conveniently, Google+ is integrated with other Google applications, such as Gmail, Google Maps and Google Calendar.

Twitter

Twitter, one of the 10 most-visited websites, is an online social networking and microblogging (very micro—only 140-character text messages) service. The short messages are called "tweets." Registered users can read and post, but everyone can read posted tweets.

As of this printing, Twitter reports there are about 284 million active users who posted more than 143,199 tweets per second. More interestingly, the site also handles 2.1 billion search queries daily. Twitter traffic tends to spike during significant events. It is a very mobile-friendly platform.

With Twitter, you can message others directly, as well as create groupings with hashtags (#) in combination with keywords about a product, event, person, city, brand or just about anything else. More on this later.

Abbreviations are common, but watch for errors that could be troublesome.

Speaking of abbreviations, Twitter allows you to conserve your 140 characters by easily shrinking links. So if you are referencing a website, the link of that site can be shrunken down to about 16 to 20 characters.

Twitter allows real-time messages that can contain photos, videos, quotes, article links and more. The tweets can receive replies and be retweeted by others who want to share your tweet with their followers.

Twitter is a resource for businesses to grow audiences, increase traffic, generate leads and have an online voice. Posting relevant and interesting tweets, linked to good content—while sharing and retweeting the content of others—will help build your audience. Twitter also offers promotion and advertising opportunities to target those folks interested in your business.

Think of Twitter as a way to search and discover content about favorite topics and people. It allows the exchange of ideas and information instantaneously, bringing folks together from around the world. Tweet as often as you like—sharing the messages that help identify your brand and the needs it helps fulfill.

Twitter is a crowded marketplace and all those followers might or might not be real—and where they come from can be suspect. Justin Bieber made news when it was reported that 38 to 52 percent of his 42 million Twitter followers—whom advertisers were paying dearly to connect with—were "bots," or computer-generated fakes. The site Status People reported that although 35 percent were likely fake and 37 percent were inactive, 28 percent were real. This still left him with close to 12 million followers, a huge audience that can be marketed to and that is likely listening closely to whatever 140-character quips he shares. The meteoric rise of Carly Rae Jepsen's song "Call Me Maybe" provided a perfect example of Twitter's power. The song is catchy for sure, but few would question the impact of Bieber's constant tweeting

ENGAGE: Smart Ideas to Get More Media Coverage,
Build Your Influence and Grow Your Business

in making Jepsen and her song overnight sensations. Only time will tell if Twitter and the power of the tweet help sustain fame and awareness.

Facebook

Facebook is a social sharing site that requires users to register and create an optional personal profile. Users can exchange messages, gather friends and receive automatic updates. Currently, Facebook boasts more than 1.23 billion users, with about nine percent of those estimated to be fake, according to Wikipedia and CNN. Fifty-three percent are female; 47 percent male. About 757 million log onto Facebook every day. Five new profiles are created every second. The relevance of this to you? It might very well be too big to ignore, and a potential audience is growing exponentially.

Users can open personal and business pages. People and posts are "liked" by Facebook users. This is a way users can show their appreciation of your posts, status updates, comments, photos or advertisements. The right to "like" whatever you like on Facebook was upheld by a federal appeals court.

You can promote your posts on Facebook to your existing followers or others who share interests similar to your general posting "themes." Between June 2012 and May 2013, 7.5 million posts were promoted, according to Facebook.

Unlike Twitter, Facebook posting is best restricted to once or twice a day so you are not overloading the feeds of your followers.

Presently, the jury is out regarding how important all those "friends" and "likes" are in the world of business. According to State of Inbound Marketing 2012, 42 percent of marketers report that Facebook is critical or important to their business. Not sure I believe that, but as with many things in life, more is likely better than less.

Instagram

Here's an amazing statistic: Instagram gets 1,000 comments per second on shared photos. I personally witnessed this when, on vacation at the beach, I befriended a young model who tagged my two children in photos within her Instagram stream. Within minutes, my tween and teen thought they were rock stars based on the number of likes and followers they accumulated.

So what is it? By its own description, Instagram is a fun and quirky way to share your life with friends through a series of pictures. You simply snap a photo with your cell phone and then choose a filter to transform the image into a memory to keep around forever.

On December 21, 2010, Instagram set a record as the quickest app to reach one million downloads. In 2014, Instagram boasts 100 million users. I'd say this is a heck of a testimonial to the app's impact.

What makes it so cool? A few things. Photo sharing is incredibly easy whether it's a new photo or one that already exists in your camera roll. Instantly you can share not only on Instagram, but also on Facebook, Twitter, Flickr and Tumblr. You can flag your photos with your location. Next, you can easily manipulate your picture. There are 11 different filters you can use, making your photos look like you spent hours in the darkroom using all sorts of professional tricks. Then, it's social. As I mentioned, people can "follow" you. They can also "like" and comment on your photos. Finding like-minded people is easy. You can see which of your Twitter and Facebook friends are using the app and easily start following them. You could load in your email address book if you're so inclined. Instagram will also suggest people whom you might like to follow. And ultimately, Instagram delivers a glimpse of the everyday lives of people from cultures all over the world. It's hard to imagine until you've seen it, but by spending time on Instagram, you'll see how people celebrate, love, appreciate, act and live the entire world over.

If you have a business that translates well into images or photos, I'd highly encourage you to consider an Instagram account.

Pinterest

Pinterest is a social networking website that allows you to organize and share ideas with others. You can share your own content as well as things that other Pinterest users have posted. Personally, for business, I think it is far superior to Instagram because it permits users to add links to a site.

Once you register for a free account, you can create your own boards to organize your content. Examples of topics include health, science, architecture, restaurants, wine, whatever. You can upload images and "pin" them to relevant boards. Other Pinterest users can browse your boards and comment on individual items. Likewise, you can browse other users' boards and "like," "repin" or comment on their pinned items.

Similar to Twitter, Pinterest allows you to follow other users. If you find another user's content to be especially interesting, you can click "Follow All" to have all their boards show up in your account in real time. If you only want to follow specific boards, you can click "Follow" next to each board you want to follow. Pinterest does not inform users when you choose to unfollow them.

StumbleUpon

I have a few apps I really like, but StumbleUpon is my all-time favorite. It is the ultimate personal education tool. StumbleUpon is a browser toolbar for Internet Explorer and Firefox. Once you open an account and declare your "interests," the tool scours the Internet for you, finding thousands of web sites or articles that match your interests. It also allows you to meet and message people with similar interests and create a network of friends. You can recommend, write reviews of, and share sites with your friends via StumbleUpon's messaging system or with anyone else via email directly from the toolbar itself.

A well-expressed StumbleUpon review stated, "From time to time, browsing the Internet can become somewhat mundane. Perhaps you have grown tired of going to the same sites all the time, and perhaps your searches have come up empty when looking for new content relative to the things you like. Maybe you wish you could meet people with similar interests and visit sites that they like to visit. StumbleUpon, in an exciting way, reinvents the web surfing experience while allowing you to do all of this. You will find yourself immersed almost immediately as you 'stumble' from site to site."

StumbleUpon recently added a new feature: each week, users get an email of "special picks" based on their interests. To date, these weekly special picks have never failed to fascinate me.

Tumblr

Tumblr debuted in 2007 as part blogging tool, part microblogging tool and part social community. Each user has his or her own tumblelog where they can publish short posts of text, images, quotes, links, video, audio and chats. You can even reblog a Tumblr post that was published on another user's tumblelog with a click of the mouse, just as you might retweet content to share it on Twitter. Furthermore, you can like other people's content on Tumblr rather than publish comments as you would on a traditional blog post. Tumblr is extremely easy to use and also works on every mobile operating system.

Your Tumblr account can be easily linked to your other social networks and you can feed your traditional blog or other RSS feed to your tumblelog. You can also create static pages such as your own questions page, that people are automatically taken to when they ask you a question. If you want to make your tumblelog private or just make specific posts private, you can. If you want to track your stats, you can add any analytics tracking code to your tumblelog, burn a feed with Feedburner, create a custom theme and use your own domain name.

In 2011, there were an estimated 20 million tumblelogs with more than five billion posts. Tumblr is free to use, so everyone from celebrities to businesspeople and politicians to teenagers are using it.

Tumblr is perfect for people who don't need a full blog to publish lengthy posts. It's also great for people who prefer to publish quick multimedia posts, particularly from their mobile devices. Tumblr is also a great choice for people who want to join a larger community. If an ongoing blog is too much or too big for you to maintain, but Twitter is too small or too inconsequential for you, then Tumblr might be just right for you.

Del.icio.us

Del.icio.us, pronounced "delicious," is a community bookmarking website in which users can save web pages they find and share them with other users. Because users' bookmarks are made public and viewable by other users, other people often bookmark web pages that they find within other users' bookmarks. Del.icio.us keeps track of how many people bookmark each site and posts the most popular websites on its home page.

Common web pages bookmarked by Del.icio.us users include news stories, online learning resources and tech support pages. Since other users add useful pages to their bookmarks, the best web pages eventually rise to the top of the popularity chain. The result is a collection of web pages that are helpful and worthwhile visiting.

Users can either browse or search the database of bookmarks on Del.icio.us. When a user saves a bookmark, he or she can add a description and tags (keywords) that are pertinent to the web page. This helps the page show up for relevant searches. The results of Del.icio.us searches are often of higher quality than a regular search engine because the sites have all been chosen by users.

Vine

A "vine" is a video, only six seconds long, of compiled clips of random stuff. They are frequently posted on social websites such as Facebook and Twitter.

With only six seconds to get your message across, you really have to plan before you start filming. Have one point you're trying to get across. Ask yourself before you start filming: what's the point of this video? What should those who view it walk away understanding? Just because it's short doesn't mean you're exempt from hammering this out; in fact, the short length makes it even *more* critical to go through this exercise. It's a lot easier to ramble than be succinct.

"Keep It Simple, Silly" if you decide to use Vine. If you need more than six seconds of footage to communicate an idea, don't forget about YouTube!

With six seconds, show your audience something about your company that's worthwhile. It could become a great way to give the public a sneak preview of a new product or service you're releasing without giving it all away.

Vine videos offer a great opportunity to humanize your company. The more human-relatable the video, the more likely somebody will find it, like it and share it—making it a win for you.

Now Let's Get Back to Our Smart Ideas for Creating Strong Social Media Content

SMART IDEA: Stop thinking about social media marketing.

There. I said it and I meant it. Stop thinking about social media marketing and stop wondering about what you think you don't know—while worrying that someone else knows more. Don't fall prey to the new PR brand of huckstership that dearly wants you to believe that they know some secret about marketing that you don't. I'm so darn sick and tired of everyone throwing around the term "social media" as if it is the be-all and end-all. It is nothing as a standalone. Marketing is an integrated, holistic set of communication solutions, and social media is but one piece of the pie.

SMART IDEA: Third-party online coverage is the best social media strategy.

Face it, 99.9 percent of what most people think of when it comes to social media is this: you go to Facebook, Twitter, Instagram, Pinterest or any other pre-established site and open a personal or company page that is basically your online bragging site. Then it is your responsibility to post new and interesting content regularly and hope people find it. Listen up: the absolute best social media program actually results when you and your company get great coverage on any page of the online outlets of traditional media. If FOX, CNN, NBC, CBS, ABC and other significant networks—or major newspapers, magazines or trades—are including you or your content anywhere on their sites, this is about as good as social media gets because of the sheer numbers in traffic these sites experience daily. This kind of coverage presence gives you priceless third-party endorsement (Yes, even if the site says "we do not endorse") in the social media setting and if you're lucky, will create backlinks to your site, which in turn improves your search engine rankings.

If you doubt me, ask anyone who is a "non-endorsed, opinions-are-their-own" *Forbes* contributor! We can refer you to the many contributors we have created. Their social and expert status raised significantly by adding "contributing *Forbes* columnist" to their resumes.

SMART IDEA: Engage.

Engage with online readers whenever and in whatever ways you can. The goal is not just to get them to read your articles or posts, but to inspire them to want to *do something with them*—whether it's sharing them or going to your website to learn more about you or your company.

If you are not engaging with your followers, you are wasting a lot of time that could be used in other more productive ways.

Engage by connecting the dots for your readers so they do more than just skim your post and move on to the next. You can captivate them.

SMART IDEA: Align your content with your goals.

Determine how you want to measure your success. It's great to have a lot of "friends" and "followers," but for business — customers and partners are much better. Social media goals should revolve around:

❖ Building traffic
❖ Creating a following
❖ Triggering interaction whether it be commentary, replies or mentions
❖ Generating revenue, relevancy, partnerships or some other value!

SMART IDEA: Listen.

Remember the "social" in social media refers to conversation. The biggest part of a conversation is listening. Nobody wants to spend time with a bore who only talks about himself. Engage your followers and listen closely to their responses.

SMART IDEA: Watch the mood.

When Twitter users are tweeting about any event that triggers emotion, particularly those deemed tragic or sad, any other discussions become irrelevant, an intrusion or simply inappropriate. Watch the trending mood based on the posts—and tread carefully if you decide to swim against it. Think three-times before making a blatant self-serving attempt to tie into it.

SMART IDEA: Identify relevant content and issues.

What industries and verticals apply to your company? How can you lead the conversation by creating content that ties you into the discussion as a thought-leader and innovator?

When you can answer those questions, hashtag (#) the industries and verticals to keep your content associated and searchable for those interested.

SMART IDEA: Determine your users' interests.

Understanding what inspires the users you seek will keep you focused on releasing content that will inspire these same users so they follow your news. If you are putting plenty of content out on the web, hopefully it is relevant. Certainly some posts will resonate much more than others. Pay attention. Ask questions. Then determine what your audience is seeking from you and lead the discussion.

SMART IDEA: Use autoposting.

A favorite app of mine is Hootsuite. It boosts social media efficiency exponentially. Hootsuite is a social media management system for brand management that makes sharing fast and very easy. The system's user interface takes the form of a dashboard and supports social network integrations for Twitter, Facebook, LinkedIn, Google+, Foursquare, MySpace, WordPress, TrendSpottr and more.

With Hootsuite, you can write a message, shrink a link, choose the platforms you want to deliver to and schedule the post to go out instantly or at some later time.

If you are managing your own social media, you want a Hootsuite account.

SMART IDEA: Beware of autoposting.

Yes, I just contradicted myself—not to be confusing but to make a point. As I said, apps like Hootsuite make the timing of your social media posts much easier. However, engagement is key. Watch the daily conversation around the web, about your competitors and regarding your industry in general. You don't have to do this 24/7/365. But popping into the chatter once in awhile lets your audiences know you are real and might trigger more meaningful connections.

The inherent convenience of autoposting is fabulous. But comment in real time on the trending news once in a while, too.

SMART IDEA: Share useful and relevant articles.

Don't post just to post. If you are reposting an old article or link, say so! "Good morning, folks! We thought this was important enough to share twice!"

SMART IDEA: Run promotions, giveaways and contests.

Offer a free product, a free trial or even a gift card to somewhere special or relevant. Trade "likes" for coupons. Trade coupons for comments. Engage your audience and give back if this kind of marketing is possible and relevant to your business products or services.

SMART IDEA: Follow industry or trade pages and then interact.

Whether by liking industry or trade posts or adding a well-thought-out comment, get on the radar screens of the other thought leaders who matter to you, your business or your industry sector.

It's kind of like back scratching: I'll scratch yours, you scratch mine. Done genuinely, the results can be fabulous.

SMART IDEA: Post pictures.

Photos added to your posts are widely estimated to receive 39 percent more interaction. KISSmetrics reports that photos get 53 percent more "likes", 104 percent more comments and 84 percent more clickthroughs. Check out Fotalia.com to buy great stock photos at very reasonable prices and choose those that are most relevant to your content, with the greatest likelihood of attracting attention. Self-explanatory photos are always best. A post with a photo will grab attention more quickly than one without. Big, bright and beautiful is the way to go. Color, black and white, dramatic, relevant…just remember add a picture whenever possible.

SMART IDEA: Follow me on…

Let everyone know there are multiple ways to receive information about your company. Twitter, YouTube, Pinterest, Instagram, Facebook, email...whatever! Each medium shows a different part of your company's personality. Let people know exactly how they can find you within each social media platform. Engage your audience on multiple levels, particularly as everyone tends to have their own personal preferences.

SMART IDEA: Show your employees in action.

When possible, post pictures that humanize your company, yet still maintain professionalism. If it is appropriate, name names and tag (#) work performance, conferences or showcases that you want to feature. Everyone likes recognition.

SMART IDEA: Let your personality shine through.

Every company has a personality. Have you thought about what yours is? Are you innovative? Seriously scientific? Trendsetting? Artistically inclined? Casual? Concerned with safety? Environmentally conscious? What is the overall impression you want people to receive when they see your corporate logo? Decide what that messaging is and make sure your posts, pictures, videos and other content reinforce your brand.

SMART IDEA: Offer a Q&A on relevant topics.

A good audience-building tactic is to remind people you are ready and willing to provide answers to their questions about your industry and your role within it. Make sure your website includes a Frequently Asked Questions (FAQ) section where you will provide more in-depth information relating to the topic already posted. Not only will users seeking information appreciate this, it will also position you and your company as a knowledgeable source of credible information.

SMART IDEA: Be prepared to screen and respond to comments to your posts.

You might not be able to respond to every comment your posts receive. However, if it's a compliment, enjoy it, thank the poster and respond with a kind comment. If it's a complaint, determine if it needs to be addressed. This might be as simple as thanking the poster for taking the time to let you know their concern. However, it might be something that warrants a review of your crisis management plan. Either way, use your social media platforms to keep tabs on your corporate health and as a way to respond and show your clients and customers that you care about their concerns.

SMART IDEA: Multiple posts per day are appropriate.

With Facebook, you don't want to post every hour, but between three to five posts per day would be enough to get your information out there without your followers hovering over the "unfriend" button. Again, skip it if the post is completely irrelevant. Even social media diehards value their time and don't want it wasted by needless noise.

SMART IDEA: Timing.

Sorry, employers, but research shows that the best hours to post your social media content coincides with the hours most people are working:

8 am to 8 pm. Highest traffic occurs between 1 pm and 3 pm. Seems lunch requires some additional "digesting."

SMART IDEA: Take advantage of holidays.

There's at least one holiday a month where you could post a relevant photo or extend greetings. Besides the usual days like Christmas, Rosh Hashanah, Thanksgiving, Veteran's Day, Memorial Day or Halloween, for example, HolidayInsights.com posts bizarre, wacky and unique holidays categorized by the month. With a bit of imagination, you could probably find at least one celebration that you can tie into each month.

SMART IDEA: Create polls.

By seeking opinions and honest feedback about your product, service or company, polls are a great way to learn more about your clients—and potential clients. You could try a simple survey on Facebook for starters if you have an audience. Otherwise, SurveyMonkey is another option that can be utilized thanks to all those emails you've hopefully been collecting. There are a variety of survey software options. Some are free but most charge a nominal fee. Come up with five relevant questions, get them out to your audience and see what the survey says!

SMART IDEA: Create CTAs.

A CTA is a clickable call to action. This could be a "Download Now," "Read More Here" or "Free Trial Here" offer. They work! It's the easiest way to direct people to where you want them to go. When designing your CTA, make sure it's not cluttered. Minimal writing in a big, bold font is best. Post CTAs on all of your social media sites and website as well. These are great ways to gather emails and more information about your audience.

SMART IDEA: Figure out what works and stick with it!

Test your posts…note which ones get more attention and figure out why. Did you use a new picture? Different wording? Use an emoticon? Tag someone? Test and retry whatever you think might be working.

SMART IDEA: Use hashtags.

When you see that # sign—that's a hashtag. You can hashtag any word that you want to align with to contribute to an overall discussion.

Hashtags make it easier to track promotional activity across many social platforms.

You can use them to start a conversation. Giving someone your website address might not start a conversation, but a hashtag before the discussion topic might make it easier.

Hashtags can be used to gently and politely inject yourself into active public conversations. Hashtags are flexible, simple and ubiquitous—so access their power by using them creatively.

Using the hashtag is the simplest way for your tweets to be found. They are acceptable in all forms of social media. Hashtag whatever words are appropriate for your industry. For example, if your company develops treatments for diabetes, every tweet that you post should have "#diabetes" in it. Then when someone uses the search tool to look up "diabetes," your posts will be shown. If you need assistance on how to use hashtags, ask any teenager. They're likely to be a pro!

SMART IDEA: Follow the trend.

On a daily basis, it might pay to take a second to review "What's Trending" on Twitter. Scroll through the topics and see if you can figure out ways to hop on the trending train. Reply, retweet or favorite to initiate conversations or piggyback onto them. Creativity, diligence and your opportunistic nature will determine your success with this rule.

SMART IDEA: Retweet!

People love to be retweeted. Not only does retweeting get you noticed by the person you retweeted, but it also exposes them to all of your followers. Retweet whatever is relevant to your audience.

SMART IDEA: Favorite.

"Favorite-ing" someone's tweet might not expose them to new audiences, but it does get you on their radar—a backdoor networking tactic that might ultimately get you an invite to the party. It's a nice way to compliment and give quick kudos. The "favorite" action is very easy. From your home timeline, simply move over the tweet you wish to favorite and select the star with the word "favorite" next to it.

SMART IDEA: Reply even when not asked.

As you scroll through Twitter, Facebook, Instagram, Pinterest or other sites, engage people in conversations even if you weren't invited. Be respectful and think through your comments before hitting the send button. Social media is about joining the public conversation. Make your posts relevant to the conversation and you might get an opportunity to showcase your expertise and/or that of your company.

SMART IDEA: Promote.

Post links to your website with a short, relevant statement about your company and add a hashtag (#) that is relevant to your industry. Do this on at least a daily basis. If you do it daily, at the end of a year, you'll have 365 industry-searchable ways to find your company.

SMART IDEA: Feed your tweets.

Feed your tweets into all of your other social media outlets: Facebook, Linked, Instagram, etc. If you use a program like Hootsuite, this is really easy. By feeding your tweets, you are creating a uniform, platform-agnostic branding campaign for your company.

SMART IDEA: Research your competition.

Notice I didn't say "follow." Rather, on a regular basis, check your "competitors" Twitter feeds to see what they have cooking. You might get some good ideas on what to do and what not to do, as well as ideas as to whom you might want to follow.

SMART IDEA: Spread out your posts.

If you decide to post 10 times a day, go for it. Just spread them out. Don't tweet everything you have to share in one hour—unless there is a timely reason for doing so. Everyone checks his or her favorite accounts at different times, and you want to optimize your chances of being seen.

SMART IDEA: Graphics tell a story.

Informational graphics are a powerful marketing tool. They are one of the easiest ways to get your content accepted as the leading professional voice of reason on any particular subject. The cool thing? You don't even have to be the source of the information or survey. Cite the work of others yet add your own take on the information, utilizing a cool design by a professional graphic artist. If done well, informational graphics are easy to understand and are more valuable than words. On Twitter, LinkedIn, Pinterest, and StumbleUpon, infographics get more shares than other posted content.

SMART IDEA: "Check it out" gets traction.

There's something behind the phrase "Check it out" that inspires action. I have no idea why. But I do know it works better than any other phrase I can think of. Suggest to your followers that they "check out" your associates, products you want to promote, sites you like—such as your very cool website!—and whatever else you think is relevant that will help your online marketing program.

SMART IDEA: Let people know how to find you online.

If you opt to have traditional social media accounts, make sure you list them on every piece of marketing material you print. Make it easy for people not only to find you, but also to be able to follow you via their preferred format.

SMART IDEA: Don't be an "egg."

By "egg," I mean the basic egg icon that is shown where a photo should be on your Twitter page. Be sure to personalize your avatar with your logo, office building, product, face…something that shares a little bit about yourself. To do otherwise is to miss a major opportunity.

SMART IDEA: Follow the experts in your field.

Follow outlets, people and experts whom you admire. Then retweet useful information from those experts to your followers. You might be surprised—one of those experts might follow you back!

SMART IDEA: Run a promotion.

Run promotions on Twitter if applicable. People love to enter contests, and they love it even more when they win! It doesn't have to be a big gift and it doesn't necessarily have to target your product. The idea is to be noticed.

SMART IDEA: Make your blog mobile-friendly.

Give visitors content they need. Carefully plan your layout, making navigation easy. Simplicity rules. Make the design work on multiple browsers and devices. Use social media icons for easier sharing. Provide links to your full site. Be mobile-ready and friendly, making usability a top priority.

SMART IDEA: Choose your online neighborhood for networking.

The average social media user has two social media accounts. Some users like to manage multiple accounts, although others find a single community and stick with it—even when the temptations of new social networks arise.

Engage and visit other outlets occasionally to check in and see where new audiences might be mingling. Poll your customers and prospects and ask them about their favorite places to network, so you too can network in all the right sites.

SMART IDEA: Outsource content development as needed.

Can your business keep up-to-date with all the tasks associated with maintaining a social presence, sharing good content, responding to users' comments and asking the questions that help engage your audience? More so, is this the best use of your staff's time? Do you really want to start learning the fine points of optimization and keyword search? Creating worthy content is time-consuming. Outsourcing brand and reputation management might be a better option. After you decide what you want to achieve, don't spread yourself too thin. Consider keeping some social outreach internal, or bring in a professional consultant for the best results. Just remember: social media is just one small aspect of an overall public relations and marketing program.

SMART IDEA: Be human.

I am the coauthor, along with my brother, of the *TurboCharged*® series of health books. We started our online presence with a content-rich website and a *TurboCharged*® Facebook page. The Facebook page initially plugged along without much of a following, as we originally posted generic content and links to an assortment of health articles. Things heated up when we started posting our meals before we ate them, our early morning exercise routines—including me in a bathrobe on a rebounder—and the recipes for whatever we cooked for dinner. This formula worked, and people started to get involved, interacting with us and bringing along their friends. Essentially, we transformed ourselves from just another two authors into accessible personalities who answered a lot of questions while sharing aspects of our lives. This "humanized" us.

How can you be more "human" in your online interactions?

SMART IDEA: Use emoticons.

Emoticons are not just for teenagers. American Express' OPEN Forum found that emoticons can make a big difference in online engagement rates. Sharing of posts is 33 percent higher; comment rates are 33 percent higher; and likes go up as much as 57 percent! Who knew what joy a silly smiley face could bring? Test some out on your next post, will ya? ;-)

SMART IDEA: Deliver a consistent brand experience.

All of your social content should mirror your website, which is your ultimate brand-building business card. Keep logos and corporate colors consistent. Maintain your message. Don't confuse your audience by trying different things for different people. Consistency is key.

SMART IDEA: Amplify in-person events with social media promotion.

A renowned concert facility that we represented in New York City does a great job encouraging attendees to share their best concert photos on the corporate Facebook and Twitter pages. You, too, can use social media to amp-up your live events by encouraging attendees to post their destination; creating an event page; exciting your crowd of followers with industry news and upcoming events; hashtagging your events as well as prominent attendees; asking attendees to vote and voice their favorite aspects of your events; streaming live video if possible; encouraging attendees to make their own mini-videos with Vine or other apps; and finally, spreading the news using traditional media as well.

SMART IDEA: Be conversational.

Social media is a conversation. So don't preach, pontificate or bore by hogging the dialogue. Be conversational. Develop your media voice and take your followers inside your brand experience. Listen to their feelings, speak their language, meet on their terms when possible and above all, communicate with authenticity and personality. This will raise the engagement level and turn fans and followers into customers and brand advocates.

SMART IDEA: Short is sweet.

Shorter posts aren't important exclusively for Twitter. Statistics show that keeping posts below 250 characters can deliver 60 percent more engagement than you might otherwise garner. Less than 80 characters can get up to 66 percent more!

SMART IDEA: Be relevant.

Readers of traditional and online media gravitate to lists of tips. Discover what you might be able to work with to make your product, company and management more relevant. For example, we represent a big brand-name coffee company. Content we create and articles we write cover topics such as organic farming, chemical-free decaffeination processes, sourcing various types of beans, right through to recipes made involving coffee! How can you create content that is meaningful to your fans and followers?

SMART IDEA: Thursdays and Fridays are the best "engagement" days.

A study by Buddy Media found that engagement on Facebook goes up 18 percent on Thursdays and Fridays. Not sure what this means for the five-day, 40-hour traditional workweek…

SMART IDEA: Ask questions.

Should, would, which, who, when, what, where, why and how are powerful online response motivators. I guess this can only mean that we all want our voices and opinions heard. Questions that have a limited answer option tend to be the highest attractors of comments. These can be simply answered with a yes or no, like or dislike, would or wouldn't, name, place or thing.

What questions can you think of that can be asked in a way that is relevant to your marketing and PR strategies?

SMART IDEA: Offer special reports.

A clever way to move traffic from your Facebook, Twitter or other social media pages to your website—which is where you really want them so they can learn more!—is to offer a special report or white paper that addresses a particular issue or problem in an interesting way.

For users to download the report, require them to go to your website. You can easily provide a link right to the download page.

SMART IDEA: Create a free course.

Is there something you can be teaching your desired partners, customers or investors? Could you break down your 100-page corporate presentation into five to 20 informative slide "classes"? If you can, this is a great way to build trust and rapport.

SMART IDEA: Educate your audience.

When posting information online, remember that you don't want to be a bore. Don't only post your news. Write posts or link to articles that elaborate on your business area or sector. Consider writing an educational series of blog posts designed to attract traffic for a competitive keyword phrase. Think issues and solutions, tips, new ways of attacking a challenge—and you'll become a thought leader rather than just an online advertiser.

SMART IDEA: Offer a free podcast.

Today, most mobile devices are built with recording capacity. Then there's the Garage Band app for more advanced recording and editing. As a result, it's easier than ever to get your message out audibly versus just via writing.

Recorded messaging is a great way to build interest in your business. You can do all the talking yourself or work with a partner in an interview format. You can record an audio version of your presentation. Or if you feel so inclined, you or your communications partner can create and record an online, downloadable education series about whatever problem or issue you want to discuss.

Become a teacher instead of a salesman and you'll build your audience.

SMART IDEA: Build a membership website.

Could your business benefit from creating a club that offers membership? Do you offer a product, service or something that could offer special opportunities for members only?

If you are a concert venue, perhaps you can offer first looks at upcoming events. A coffee shop—a free cup for subscribing. A tech company—a private newsletter that explores new innovations in the industry. A biotech company serving an audience with unmet medical needs could provide a patient advocacy chatroom for members only.

Think about your product, service or offering. What exclusive information or offer can you make to your audience in exchange for their email address? (Which of course you will treasure like gold, as you will use it judiciously for future marketing purposes!)

SMART IDEA: All content should reflect your business vision.

Whenever you post a blog, write an article or contribute to an online forum discussing your business topic, remember that your answers are content. Make sure this content reflects well on you.

You can adjust the content to the site's audience, and you should. Consumers, for example, might benefit from more analogies or story-telling and possibly even a dose of humor, whereas scientists might like in-depth details that are…deeply scientific. Gauge accordingly and post away!

SMART IDEA: Multiply your most popular blog posts.

Pay attention to what content gets the greatest response. When you notice that a topic resonates, maximize its impact. Could you add some really good images and translate it into PowerPoint? Make a YouTube video? Send a newsletter by snail mail to your mailing list?

Or maybe you can add a sequel to the topic. Maybe you can convert its format and disseminate the article to a larger audience via a traditional newswire and possibly see coverage in print, radio, television/cable and other Internet outlets.

Pay attention to your content that starts a conversation. Then make more news with that news, following many of the steps in this book.

SMART IDEA: Offer a solution to a problem.

Whenever you can discuss how you've overcome a difficult problem, you will build credibility and a larger audience. We touched upon this when I talked about being "human." Don't fall into the trap of thinking you have to be an infallible guru. Instead, share in a way that shows you to be a real person who has solved problems that your readers will find relevant.

SMART IDEA: Aggregate your content and repurpose it.

Whenever you appear in the media, whether in print, online or on TV, keep clippings of your coverage in a safe place. Then, on a regular basis—or whenever you want to reach out to an existing or new audience—send out your clips in electronic or traditional format with a letter describing the coverage. This will build your status as a thought leader who is in demand by the media. Sharing these third-party endorsements will put you ahead of the competition when someone is trying to decide if they want to do business with you or invest in your company.

SMART IDEA: Host a virtual conference.

People often don't attend conferences—even though they would love to learn more about a topic of interest—because the logistics of travel are just too challenging.

However, there is nothing stopping you from sharing the same information and helping your desired audience by incorporating virtual conferences into your communications mix.

Gather four to five of the most educated people on your topic and create a virtual conference. Each presenter can give a five to 15-minute audio or video workshop.

Virtual conferences are a relatively simple way to create a marketable event.

SMART IDEA: Even your comments are content.

When you are surfing the web, trolling through websites that interest you and feeling the urge to comment, remember this: your comments on other people's blogs are content. Respect this and treat your entire online dialogue as content. Anything you post online is likely to remain on the Internet indefinitely, be forever searchable and therefore traceable right back to you and your company. Treat your comments as content. Strive to be original, relevant and interesting.

SMART IDEA: Be complimentary to others in your peer group.

In the competitive world of business, you can actually gain an audience by complimenting and singing the praises of others you admire. Genuinely compliment and acknowledge the good things others do. By doing so, you will benefit in a number of ways. First, you will become tied to someone else's news, even though you had nothing to do with it except for nicely noticing it. Second, many partnerships, both formal and informal, can be forged as a result of kind words. Kindness will always multiply your success.

SMART IDEA: Create a buyer's guide.

An online buyer's guide allows you to frame purchasing questions on your terms. You can address concerns not only relating to your product, but also how your product stacks up against the competition.

Let buyers know what to watch out for and pay attention to. Give them the questions they should be asking.

Make your buyer's guide real—and consider throwing in compliments for your competitors. Doing this will build your credibility and help the guide go viral.

For example, on the *TurboCharged*® website, blogs and social media pages created by my brother and I, we often reference articles by other health book writers. Although we might not always agree with everything they are saying, there's plenty to compliment that is common sense and good for everyone's health. Often we're both surprised and flattered when Dr. Oz, Dr. Fred Pescatore and Dr. Joe Mercola compliment, reference and follow our news back.

SMART IDEA: It doesn't have to be called your "blog."

On the Dian Griesel Int'l. website, we call our blog The Big Orange. We share juicy news and the orange reinforces our signature color.

You don't have to call your blog a blog either. It's your child! Give it a name. Maybe, for example, it's The Tech Plant, The Concert Hall, The Discovery Lab or The Jeweler's Corner. In addition to the name, is it a virtual concierge of information? An industry-related tutorial? A trade gossip column? An industry e-school? A trade-term dictionary? An industry/event directory?

Name your "blog" so that it inspires interaction and/or return visitors.

SMART IDEA: Write a manifesto.

If something within your industry needs to be addressed, be bold and write a manifesto. Maybe you want to allude to it in your blog posts in a variety of social media outlets and offer it only to those who specifically request a copy.

But rant and rave about the issue and why it simply MUST be addressed. Create a movement. Become the voice willing to speak out and ask the questions that are not being asked.

SMART IDEA: Become a reviewer.

Sometimes the easiest way to create content is by reviewing the books, blogs, newsletters, tools, products and information of others.

If you are regularly reading—and you *must* be—you'll find plenty of things that you can compliment, recommend or trash. I realize it's hard to believe, but people actually search the Internet seeking the opinions of others before making many decisions. Why not get your name out there as a voice of reason?

SMART IDEA: Create "Top," "Best" and "Must" lists.

If the Internet and modern society could be accused of having one major flaw, it might be "too much information."

Before making certain decisions, many of us go to the Internet to search for opinions, ideas and competitor offerings, and it is easy to be overwhelmed.

Expert that you are, you can take advantage of this information over-load phenomenon and help others! Start by creating lists of: "The Five Best Ways to _____" or "The Top 10 Ways to _____".

Be concise, simple, user-friendly without jargon, and move your readers through the information abyss.

SMART IDEA: Tie your product or service to a celebrity.

Some celebrity is always doing something weird and newsworthy. If people are talking, you have an opportunity to tie into the news if you're creative.

What are five things your business has in common with…Giselle Bundchen (you both like football players), Elvis Presley (your fans think you're still alive even after you had a high-profile crisis), Steve Jobs (you're both innovators), Bill Gates (you're an innovator who is also trying to save the world), Warren Buffett (your product/technology/service fits his investing strategy), Paris Hilton (you have nothing in common—except you like to be in the news!).

Call me if you need an idea. I guarantee I can come up with not just the headline, but also the perfect photo to make your online story gain lots of traction. Just ask me how we worked a series of stories about a new American Psychiatric Society term, Jack LaLanne and Alec Baldwin to our ultimate benefit and profit!

SMART IDEA: Seek inspiration from Digg.

Find a headline that has nothing to do with you and turn it around, tying your company into it. For example, a while back, a Digg story that was trending high (no pun intended) was titled: "Why You See What You See When You're Tripping on Psychedelic Drugs." At my firm, we represented a company that was formulating a nonaddictive formula for oxycodone. Not an exact tie-in—but we used this hot story to point out the problems of drug addiction and what our client company was developing to address this serious issue. The result was that our client was featured in major traditional television outlets, newspapers and magazines, and the story went viral.

SMART IDEA: Follow like-minded people in your industry.

I admit I am two-faced about this rule: I allow almost anyone to become my friend on Facebook. Thankfully, there are some real friends in there too, among the strangers! I also very selectively follow certain people who I think will help me learn more about certain industries.

However, when it comes to LinkedIn, I am highly selective as to who gets into my network, for two reasons:

1. Often people will ask for a reference regarding someone, based on the fact that they see I am linked to that person. If I wouldn't provide a glowing reference, I won't link.
2. If I don't want certain people trolling my online associates for business, I don't link to them.

Follow this rule as it fits your own online strategies.

SMART IDEA: Be educational.

By offering content that others find helpful, you'll become an authority in your field. I find it ironic that the more I freely share what I know in articles, books, blogs and conversations, the more people think I know. This creates an interesting cycle: I am compelled to keep learning more because I'd hate to feel like an imposter or have to admit that I have reached my peak of knowledge! I don't want to stop learning and expanding my knowledge base, ever. In fact, I'd like to keep learning, writing and sharing after I die! I am hoping there's a way I can get some relevant messages back to people I know and love.

SMART IDEA: Remember entertainment value.

Occasional light humor, harmless gossip and banter can go a long way toward humanizing your brand. What can you share that ups the entertainment quotient of your feed?

SMART IDEA: Throw in some inspiration.

Inspiring quotes and photos are a good way to keep you and your brand "humanized." Don't preach. Rather, make your quotes—with or without cool images— reflective and inspirational.

SMART IDEA: Create a useful tool.

Is there a checklist, spreadsheet-based calculator, cheat sheet or planning worksheet that can be distributed to your blog subscribers or email list? These make great "thank yous" for subscribing to your site.

There is nary an industry that cannot come up with some sort of guide to surviving, thriving, living, growing, learning or succeeding better within that industry. How can you offer a free tool that helps others?

SMART IDEA: Try gratitude.

On random or certain special days like Valentine's Day or Thanksgiving, be grateful and thank your subscribers, fans, followers and friends. It's impossible to remind people too often that we are grateful for knowing them, working with them and collaborating with them. Maybe you can create special "gratitude content" for subscribers only. The goal here is to thank your constituents for their attention and business. If there is some way you can post and fulfill a simple reward for your followers, this is a great time to do it. Jet Blue, for example, has $59 fare days. What can you offer to say thanks?

SMART IDEA: Get crazy and gain followers.

Depending upon what kind of audience/consumers/partners you

are trying to attract, you might want to post a series or a regular column "authored" by your child, your dog, your cat, your bird or your pet iguana. As talented as she is, Lady Gaga might not have been propelled so quickly into the music limelight without a little craziness. For starters, she named her fans "monsters" and they liked it!

Explore your inner crazy. Sometimes a test or two is your best strategy.

SMART IDEA: Make an absurd comparison.

The further you have to reach, the better it will work. Some of my favorite business columns are based on reaches. You could author an industry advice piece based around one of the following headlines:

* ❖ What Not To Do in Interviews as Learned from the Housewives of...
* ❖ How SpongeBob Taught Me to...
* ❖ Lessons Learned from Exploitation Queen Kim Kardashian
* ❖ What Arnold Schwarzenegger and X have in Common...
* ❖ What the INDY 500 has in common with...

CHAPTER 15:

Getting "Buy" with a Little Help from Your "Friends": A Special Chapter for Publicly Traded Companies

In my book *FUNDaMentals: The Corporate Guide to Cultivating Investor Mindshare*, I focused on the unique investor relations challenges of smaller and lesser-known publicly traded companies.

Engage would be incomplete if I didn't devote some space again to the unique needs of Fair Disclosure for publicly traded companies and what I view as the current divide between established wire services and social media platforms.

The issue of wire service dissemination versus social media dissemination received significant attention back in the mid-2000s, when the CEO of publicly traded Sun Microsystems, Jonathan Schwartz, challenged the Securities and Exchange Commission, claiming the Sun website was active enough with users that press releases posted there would be compliant and represent full disclosure. This challenge, fostered by others and the rise of various social media platforms, sparked a debate as to whether it was really necessary to pay for an established wire service for news dissemination.

Almost a decade later, despite the meteoric rise of Twitter, Facebook, Instagram and other outlets, I would still advise a publicly traded company to issue their material news releases via one of the nationally recognized wire services. Someday my opinion might change, but frankly, getting nailed for inadequate dissemination and getting served with a shareholder lawsuit making that claim, is reason enough to stick with the status quo. This said, the status quo would benefit from being complemented with active online media outreach.

The smart idea below is a full excerpt of a press release disseminated by Business Wire, a Berkshire Hathaway company, on April 4, 2013. I can't say it any better, so with permission and full credit, I'm acknowledging the entire release as a smart idea.

SMART IDEA: Social media platforms are only one component of full and fair disclosure for publicly traded companies.

Although Business Wire stated that it is strongly supportive of social media tools, web posting on company websites, and blogging as supplemental platforms to communicate material information, the company believes that a broadly disseminated news release—distributed simultaneously and in real-time via a legitimate newswire service—is still the most effective way to maximize investor outreach, and to inclusively serve the needs of all market participants.

In Business Wire's view, the SEC's latest guidance on the possible standalone use of social media platforms for regulatory compliance purposes poses a disservice to the investment community, threatening increased fragmentation of price-sensitive information, privacy concerns as users are required to register to gain access to material news, security risks that might adversely affect market stability, and the loss of simultaneity—and the "level playing field"—that is at the core of Regulation Fair Disclosure.

Business Wire, which makes extensive use of Twitter (with 61 industry Twitter feeds) and other social media tools as part of its multichannel distribution platform, believes that social media should be leveraged as part of a broader news dissemination strategy. Reliance on social media alone, even in accordance with the SEC's newly issued guidelines, will likely negatively impact market fairness and investor awareness.

However, social media used in conjunction with Reg FD-compliant disclosure vehicles, including a broadly circulated news release, an 8-K filing, and an IR website, is a valuable adjunct that extends the reach of investor communications. "Best Practices" dictate that investor relations professionals utilize the full ensemble of communications tools at their disposal.

"Protecting our clients' sensitive information is at the core of what we do, and we'll continue to do that in the most secure and innovative way possible," said Cathy Baron Tamraz, Business Wire's chairwoman and CEO, in a news release. "Social media can be a valuable part of the investor relations ecosystem, but it should not be the core. Social media has been an integral part of our distribution platform for many years, and we also hold two social media patents. However, we are wary of unintended consequences by limiting access to a single site that doesn't have the security, reliability or interface to reliably serve the entire investment community."

In a Business Wire blog post, the company's SVP of global marketing,

Thomas Becktold, offered the following list of social media opportunities and cautions for companies:

Social Media Opportunities for Public Companies

❖ Social media channels offer the ability to gather intelligence and engage in two-way conversations, and as part of a comprehensive communications mix, are quite valuable.

❖ Companies should establish official IR-specific social media channels on key platforms, even if they are not ready to use them. If the channels are not active, put a disclaimer or keep them dark.

❖ For those with a solid understanding of social media and their investor audiences, regular, consistent use of the channels for both good news and bad news is key. Just like any other disclosure platform, don't tweet or post only the good results and skip the bad ones. Once you commit to adding a social media channel to your communications mix, stick to it. If you discontinue use of a channel, communicate that as well.

❖ Establish and publish a clear policy on your company's use of social media as a supplemental channel to alert investors of disclosure press releases and filings. Cross-reference those channels on your IR site, press releases and filings.

❖ Listen to conversations and track sentiment and influencers, including your company's Twitter "Cash Tag"—tweets tagged with your ticker symbol preceded by a $. Business Wire now offers social media sentiment analysis reports for press releases via its partnership with NUVI. For real-time monitoring and engagement, the NUVI platform provides an easy visual representation of influencers and sentiment based on the terms you choose.

Social Media Cautions for Public Companies

❖ Full and Fair Access: According to Pew Research as reported by TechCrunch, only 16 percent of adult online users are using Twitter.

❖ Privacy: Social media channels have barriers to entry and require the user to set up accounts and agree to the terms and conditions of each channel. Your company does not control those terms and they might be objectionable to those interested in your news. Chances are likely that your own IR site as a best practice, does not require visitors to agree to terms and conditions to access material news.

❖ Fragmentation: *Where's Waldo* meets disclosure. As an IRO, do you opt for a wide, instantaneous Business Wire distribution or solely post to Twitter or Facebook and hope people find your material information? Ask yourself, how do your investors, potential investors and media currently access your news? Chances are, it's through a widely divergent set of sources.

❖ Simultaneity: The fact that users must click on a link to read a full-text announcement that will reside elsewhere adds latency and unfairness to the disclosure process.

❖ Usability: Is social media going to meet the needs of your audiences? Is it realistic to ask your institutional investors to hit "Like" on Facebook to get the latest earnings release alongside their elementary school friend's picture of their latest cake or new puppy? Should you expect your retail investor to stop relying on their brokerage account to access your news because it's no longer there and instead subscribe to your Twitter feed?

❖ Security: Don't use social media as your sole means for disclosure. Look at Kevin Ware, the Louisville basketball player, and what happened on Twitter just after his on-court accident. Someone set up a fake account because, yes, we know it's that easy to do. And that fake account had more followers than his real account. Imagine potential investors searching in vain for the "real" Twitter account for your company when breaking news happens. Or finding the official account has been hacked, as happened to both Burger King and Jeep. Want to get a "verified" account? Good luck—and it might not make a difference anyway, according to a Mashable article. The Business Wire slug ensures a seamless, secure, audited experience.

❖ Reliability: Twitter has been riddled with outages as it grows— think how many times you've seen the Fail Whale. Business Wire operates at more than 99 percent uptime. With your news widely distributed, if one site or system goes down, investors have many others to turn to.

❖ Liability: Leveraging a Business Wire distribution ensures full and fair distribution. Tweeting a release today is akin to walking across a frozen lake in late March. Your odds of making it across are good, not great.

Conclusion

Thanks for staying with me this far and reading my book to the end. I hope I have made you aware of all—or at least most—of what you need to know to effectively engage with the media and achieve the public relations results you want.

Good public relations campaigns will:

- ❖ Create awareness of your company
- ❖ Build credibility for your company and its products or services
- ❖ Increase leads and sales among existing and prospective customers
- ❖ Set the stage for future fundraising
- ❖ Attract prospective business partners or strategic alliances
- ❖ Position your company for mergers or acquisitions
- ❖ Keep your company in the minds and portfolios of investors

When I meet with a management team seeking representation and the subject of public relations comes up, I often hear expressions of dismay at previous relationships with public relations companies. Their experience reminds me of the following tale:

One day while walking down the street, a highly successful public relations executive was hit by a bus and died instantly. Her soul arrived in heaven, where St. Peter himself met her at the Pearly Gates. "Welcome to Heaven," said St. Peter. "But before you get settled it seems we have a problem. Strangely enough, we've never had a public relations executive make it this far and we're not sure what to do with you." "No problem, just let me in," said the woman. "Well, I'd like to, but I have higher orders," said St. Peter. "What we're going to do is let you have a day in Hell and a day in Heaven. Then you can choose where you want to spend eternity." "Actually, I think I've made up my mind. I would prefer to stay in Heaven," said the woman. "Sorry, we have rules," St. Peter responded, and with that he put the executive in an elevator that quickly descended to Hell. The doors opened and the PR executive found herself stepping out of the elevator onto the putting green of a beautiful golf course. In the distance was a country club. Standing in front of her were all of the friends and fellow executives with whom she had worked. They were all dressed in evening finery and cheering for her. They ran up and kissed her on both cheeks and talked about old times. She played an excellent round of golf, and at night went to the country club where she enjoyed a delicious steak and lobster dinner. She met the Devil who was actually a nice guy and kind of cute. She had a great time telling jokes and dancing. All too soon it was time to leave. Everybody waved goodbye as she got on the elevator, which went up and opened at the Pearly Gates, where she found St. Peter awaiting her arrival. "Now it's time to spend a day in Heaven," he said. So she spent the next 24 hours lounging around on clouds, playing the harp and singing, and had a great time. Before she knew it, her 24 hours were up, and St. Peter came and got her. "You've spent a day in Hell and you've spent a day in Heaven. Now you must choose your eternity," he said. The woman paused for a second and then replied, "Well, I never thought I'd say this. I mean, Heaven has been great and all, but I had a better time in Hell." St. Peter escorted her to the elevator, and again she went back down to Hell. When the doors of the elevator opened she found herself standing in a desolate wasteland covered in garbage and filth. She saw her friends dressed in rags, picking through the garbage and filling sacks. The Devil came over and put his arm around her. "I don't understand," stammered the woman. "Yesterday there was a golf course and a country club. We ate lobster and danced and had a great time. Now there's this wasteland of garbage and my friends all look miserable." "Yes," said the Devil, smiling at her. "As a public relations executive you should understand. Yesterday we were pitching to you. Today you're a client."

This is NOT how I view our public relations responsibilities at my company! But too often, the management teams of companies I meet with, initially complain that in the past they have shelled out high fees for PR, yet received too few results. Consequently, it is understandable that they have wondered if PR is simply a bottomless money pit. This is sad, because the fact is that, when thoughtfully initiated, public relations programs are extremely valuable tools—especially for small or underfollowed companies. If the person or firm you have hired is not providing thoughtful, wise counsel and not getting your story into the appropriate print or broadcast media, hire someone else.

With creativity, imagination and perseverance, any company, product, venture or person can get media coverage. I can tell you that my company has successfully placed feature stories for previously "unknown" companies and people in outlets like *Fortune, Time, Bloomberg Businessweek, The Wall Street Journal and The New York Times*, along with hundreds of other regional daily newspapers and thousands of trade publications. Our CEOs have also appeared on national and regional television affiliates and other cable and radio business programs and segments. The secret to securing placements is relentless perseverance coupled with energetic enthusiasm. It is also essential to have excellent writing skills and an understanding of what editors and producers want for various audiences.

Beware of firms that tell you they have "excellent media contacts." The media are ready to hear any newsworthy or trend-based story if it's a good one. Don't expect your story to hit prime time until you have spent the time to shape and promote it...or hired a qualified firm to do this for you.

If you want to pitch your story on your own, keep this book handy. It covers pretty much everything you need to know for success. However, if you find you'd like professional help with your company's corporate communications program, feel free to call me.

I can be reached at:
DGriesel@DGIcomm.com
Dian Griesel Int'l.
335 West 38th Street, 3rd Floor
New York, NY 10018

Telephone: 212.825.3210
or
Dian Griesel Int'l.
P.O. Box 302
Washington Depot, CT 06794

www.diangriesel.com
www.DGIcomm.com
www.DGIwire.com
Twitter.com/diangriesel
Facebook.com/diangrieselinc
Pinterest.com/diangriesel
LinkedIn.com Dian Griesel, Ph.D.
Twitter.com/DGIwire

Facebook.com/DGIwire

Pinterest.com/DGIwire

About
Dian Griesel

For more than 30 years, companies and select individuals have sought Dian Griesel's candid perspective and practical advice concerning a variety of projects, situations and circumstances. A lifelong serial entrepreneur and media commentator, she has founded several businesses in addition to Dian Griesel International, which she currently serves as President. Her predecessor company, The Investor Relations Group, grew over 16 years to become an award-winning, multimillion dollar revenue communications firm that was purchased by an investment bank. Prior, Dian—a Ph.D. in nutritional sciences—was in private practice and a frequent "expert" guest on many of the talk shows that film in New York City. Throughout the 1980s, Dian worked in entertainment. She started by assisting publicist icon Judy Katz in publicizing Power Station recording studios, owned by the legendary Tony Bongiovi and Bob Walters. Dian moved on to form Stand Up and Rock, an entertainment agency booking bands and comedians for the college circuit. Later she formed a new sister company to Spotlite Entertainment, co-partnering with Robert Williams, Spotlite's entertainment mogul founder, to form Spotlite Marketing, where she had the opportunity to market corporate sponsorship deals for clients Jay Leno, Jerry Seinfeld, Yakov Smirnoff and many other top-tier acts.

Dian is the author of several financial presentation books including *FUNDaMentals: The Corporate Guide to Cultivating Investor Mindshare*. Together with *Engage*, these two books address how to utilize the best of traditional communication techniques while understanding what social media is, what it can realistically deliver, the value of concise messaging for the best return on investment, and the strategic implementation of news flow that communicates to all of your audiences via their preferred distribution mediums.

Dian is also the cofounder of a publishing company, The Business School of Happiness, and coauthor of the *TurboCharged*® series of books and downloads written specifically for busy people seeking greater health and peak performance in all aspects of their lives. Dian has served on several boards including the New York Chapter of the American Heart Association and The Rumsey Hall School. She is also a business, media and health expert who appears regularly in print and on broadcast outlets. She is married, has a tween and teen, meditates daily, and enjoys treasure hunting.